Great Taste ~ Low Fat

STIR-FRIES & SAUTÉS

TIME
LIFE
BOOKS

ALEXANDRIA, VIRGINIA

Beef and Broccoli Lo Mein

page 59

Fish & Shellfish

INTRODUCTION

Our mission at Great Taste-Low Fat is to take the work and worry out of everyday low-fat cooking; to provide delicious, fresh, and filling recipes for family and friends; to use quick, streamlined methods and available ingredients; and, within every recipe, to keep the percentage of calories from fat under 30 percent.

Although the term "flash in the pan" arises from early photography methods, it's an apt description for a cooking method long used in both Eastern and Western cuisines. This essential technique—cooking food quickly in an uncovered pan while stirring to keep it from sticking—is called "stir-frying" if the pieces of food are small enough to be constantly mixed and tossed; the term "sauté" is applied to larger pieces, such as turkey or pork cutlets or fish fillets.

THE WOK AND SKILLET

Even though a Chinese cook seems to work magic with a huge, fire-blackened wok, and a French chef would be lost without a hefty copper or steel *sauteuse,* you don't really need any special equipment for these recipes. A large, sturdy nonstick skillet, along with your favorite nonstick spatula or cooking spoon, is all you need for both the stir-fries and sautés in this book. (For more information on cooking equipment, see pages 6–7).

In another break with tradition, we've made our recipes considerably more healthful by reducing the amount of cooking fat used: A classic stir-fry or sauté calls for 2 to 4 tablespoons of fat for four servings (Asian cooks mostly use oil, while European sautés are cooked in clarified butter or a mixture of butter and oil). When using a nonstick pan, however, you can cook an entrée for four in just 1 to 4 teaspoons of fat. Using highly poly- and monounsaturated oils (such as safflower or olive oil) in such modest amounts keeps your meals healthy.

WHY STIR-FRY?

Stir-frying and sautéing are made to order for busy families. Our chef, Sandy Gluck, often relies on these techniques for weekday dinners for her husband and son. "Not only is stir-frying fast, but since it's a stovetop technique, it doesn't heat up the kitchen," notes Sandy. "If I have time the night before, I like to cut up the vegetables in advance. Sometimes I even measure and mix dry ingredients, such as the flour and seasonings for a dredging mixture or a combination of dried herbs called for in a recipe." Her professional experience has made orderly, methodical cooking a habit. "In classic Chinese cooking—and in the French tradition, too—you need to have all the ingredients lined up and ready to go into the pot before you start cooking. We've all seen chefs work this way on television cooking shows, but it's not just for looks: It's the most efficient and foolproof way to cook, because you're sure to add things in the correct order, and it's hard to leave anything out by accident." Stir-fries and sautés can be varied slightly according to the availability and quality of the ingredients in your market. Substitutions may be made in pasta shapes, vegetables, and herbs, if you use common sense to make the exchanges.

A WIDE WORLD OF FLAVORS

Although stir-fries are thought of as Chinese, and sautés are classically French, both techniques can be adapted to a wealth of ingredients. So along with the Chinese-style dishes in this book, you'll find recipes for Thai-Style Chicken and Vegetables, an Indian-flavored Curried Vegetable Stir-Fry, and Japanese-inspired Stir-Fried Swordfish Teriyaki. Because Mexican and Italian food are so popular, we've included Vegetable Fajitas as well as Sautéed Chicken with Pesto Fettuccine, and Pan-Fried Ravioli with Vegetables. In addition to casual French dishes like Ratatouille Stir-Fry with Goat Cheese, there are Greek, German, and Middle Eastern recipes to choose from. Closer to home, we've updated some American favorites, including Pepper Steak Stir-Fry, Beef and Mushroom Burgers, and Chicken Creole.

So if frying had become a forbidden word at your house—think again. Get out your wok or skillet and use these two time-honored cooking techniques to bring an irresistible variety of healthful international meals to the table.

CONTRIBUTING EDITORS

Sandra Rose Gluck*, a New York City chef, has years of experience creating delicious low-fat recipes that are quick to prepare. Her secret for satisfying results is to always aim for great taste and variety. By combining readily available, fresh ingredients with simple cooking techniques, Sandra has created the perfect recipes for today's busy lifestyles.*

Grace Young *has been the director of a major test kitchen specializing in low-fat and health-related cookbooks for over 12 years. Grace oversees the development, taste testing, and nutritional analysis of every recipe in Great Taste-Low Fat. Her goal is simple: take the work and worry out of low-fat cooking so that you can enjoy delicious, healthy meals every day.*

Kate Slate *has been a food editor for almost 20 years, and has published thousands of recipes in cookbooks and magazines. As the Editorial Director of Great Taste-Low Fat, Kate combined simple, easy to follow directions with practical low-fat cooking tips. The result is guaranteed to make your low-fat cooking as rewarding and fun as it is foolproof.*

NUTRITION

Every recipe in *Great Taste-Low Fat* provides per-serving values for the nutrients listed in the chart at right. The daily intakes listed in the chart are based on those recommended by the USDA and presume a nonsedentary lifestyle. The nutritional emphasis in this book is not only on controlling calories, but on reducing total fat grams. Research has shown that dietary fat metabolizes more easily into body fat than do carbohydrates and protein. In order to control the amount of fat in a given recipe and in your diet in general, no more than 30 percent of the calories should come from fat.

Nutrient	Women	Men
Fat	<65 g	<80 g
Calories	2000	2500
Saturated fat	<20 g	<25 g
Carbohydrate	300 g	375 g
Protein	50 g	65 g
Cholesterol	<300 mg	<300 mg
Sodium	<2400 mg	<2400 mg

These recommended daily intakes are averages used by the Food and Drug Administration and are consistent with the labeling on all food products. Although the values for cholesterol and sodium are the same for all adults, the other intake values vary depending on gender, ideal weight, and activity level. Check with a physician or nutritionist for your own daily intake values.

SECRETS OF LOW-FAT COOKING

STIR-FRIES AND SAUTÉS

Few cooking techniques allow for as much variety as stir-frying and sautéing; but whatever the ingredients, the basic techniques remain the same. In sautéing, cutlets, fish fillets, or chunky vegetables are placed in a hot pan to be quickly browned; you occasionally shake the pan or use a spatula to move the food about and keep it from sticking. A stir-fry is a livelier undertaking, with the small-cut ingredients being tossed and stirred from the moment they hit the pan.

THE TIME FACTOR

In a mixed stir-fry or sauté—one in which, for example, several different vegetables plus meat, poultry, or seafood are cooked together—each ingredient must be timed so it's perfectly cooked and not overcooked: Dense vegetables like turnips and parsnips take longer to become crisp-tender than delicate sugar snap peas, zucchini, and the like. We accommodate these variations in two ways: First, you can cook the various ingredients one at a time, removing each one from the pan as it's done. We often use this method for meat, poultry, and fish, which are stir-fried or sautéed until cooked through, then set aside, to be returned to the pan after the other ingredients are cooked.

You can also add the ingredients to the pan cumulatively in a logical order, beginning with those that require the longest cooking and gradually adding the quicker-cooking foods; flavoring vegetables, such as onions and garlic, often go in first. For example, in our Stir-Fried Swordfish Teriyaki (page 138), the scallions, garlic, and ginger are cooked until fragrant, then the mushrooms and carrots are added. The swordfish goes in next, and the delicate snow peas are added last.

THE FINER POINTS

Cutting ingredients into small or thin pieces (see page 8) exposes more surface area to the heat for faster cooking. It also helps the food to become more thoroughly coated with seasonings, and allows for more all-over browning (which enhances flavor, especially in meat, poultry, and fish).

To brown properly and not create excess steam, foods to be sautéed or stir-fried must be dry. Meat, poultry, and fish are often dredged with flour or cornstarch to create a dry surface: Sometimes herbs and spices are added to the dredging mixture for extra flavor.

Wok cooking is traditionally done over very high heat, but with their minimal amounts of oil, our recipes should be stir-fried over medium heat.

Still, the food should sizzle as it hits the pan. When our recipes say to add ingredients to the pan and stir-fry, keep the pan over the heat, tossing the ingredients with a spatula or spoon and shaking the pan occasionally.

CHOOSE YOUR TOOLS

Any stir-fry or sauté recipe in this book can be prepared in a large nonstick skillet—large, because if the pieces of food are crowded together, steam will be trapped and the food will turn out soggy rather than delicately crisp. For stir-fries, you have the option of using a nonstick wok, the Chinese pot developed for this cooking technique: Its wide, bowl-like shape is ideal for stir-frying. Whichever you choose, a good quality utensil makes cooking more efficient and pleasant.

A wok should be big enough (at least 12 inches across) to allow for vigorous tossing and stirring, and must conduct heat evenly without hot spots. A round-bottomed wok works best on a gas range: Its bowl-like base will rest in the burner, letting the flame rise along the sides. If you have an electric stove, a flat-bottomed wok will stand steady on the flat burner and heat evenly. Round-bottom woks are often sold with a metal ring that can be placed around the burner, allowing the wok to be used on either a gas or electric range.

Your nonstick skillet should be 10 to 12 inches across, of heavy-gauge steel or aluminum with a flat bottom. A handle that doesn't conduct heat is a plus—otherwise, you'll have to hold the pan with a potholder as you cook.

Nonstick finishes have been greatly improved since they were first invented, and today's nonstick pans are extremely durable. If your old skillet is badly scratched (or if it tends to scratch easily), you may want to replace it with one of the newer models. Just to be safe, always use smooth nylon, plastic, or wooden spatulas and spoons on nonstick pans; they're gentler on the finish than metal utensils.

Since there's considerable slicing, dicing, and chopping involved in making stir-fried and sautéed dishes, you'll want to be prepared with a generously sized cutting board and a sturdy, well-sharpened 8- to 10-inch chef's knife. A stack of small bowls or custard cups—nothing fancy, the cheapest will do—is useful for holding your prepared ingredients.

TECHNIQUES FOR QUICK AND EVEN COOKING

For sautéing and stir-frying, foods that are to be cooked together should be of a uniform size. For speedy cooking, the pieces should be either small or thin—or both.

For sautéing, this means that meat and poultry are sliced thin, and sometimes pounded to flatten the meat into a thin cutlet or scallop. (Fish steaks and fillets, and shrimp and scallops, are already just right for pan-cooking.) Vegetables for a sauté may be sliced, diced, or julienne-cut.

For stir-frying, the ingredients are usually cut quite small: Meat, poultry, and thick cuts of fish may be cut into cubes or strips. Thin vegetables such as bell peppers are cut into strips or squares, while solid vegetables like sweet potatoes or carrots may be sliced or julienned. Cutting vegetables crosswise on a diagonal exposes more surface area for quicker cooking.

Our recipes call for lean cuts of meat that are cut very thin and cooked quickly. The quick-cooking keeps the meat juicy, and cutting it into small pieces tenderizes it by shortening the meat fibers. Chilling the meat before cutting it firms up the texture, making it easier to slice: Fifteen minutes in the freezer will do the trick.

Pounding

A boneless chicken breast half is naturally thicker at one side. To even it out a bit, place the chicken breast between two sheets of plastic wrap or waxed paper. Pound the thicker side lightly with a meat pounder or the flat side of small skillet.

To make quick-cooking cutlets from boneless pork chops, place the chops between two sheets of plastic wrap or waxed paper and with a meat pounder or the flat side of a small skillet, pound the chops to a ¼- to ⅛-inch thickness.

Diagonal Slicing

Cutting long, slender vegetables—especially hard vegetables that require longer cooking times—such as carrots and parsnips, on the diagonal exposes more surface area to the heat for quicker cooking; it also gives the slices an appealing oval shape.

Cutting Chicken Strips

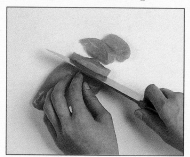

This is how to cut the chicken when the recipe calls for "chicken breasts cut crosswise into ½-inch-wide strips" (crosswise means across the grain). For easier cutting, chill the chicken breasts in the freezer for about 15 minutes first.

Cutting Beef Strips

To cut the very thin strips of meat called for in our stir-fry recipes, first chill the steak in the freezer for about 15 minutes to make it firmer. Then with a long, sharp knife, cut the steak in half horizontally, using a careful sawing motion.

Separate the two pieces of meat and return them briefly to the freezer, if necessary, to refirm them. Then cut each piece crosswise (across the grain) into thin strips; our recipes call for strips that are either ⅛ or ¼ inch thick.

CHICKEN & TURKEY

1

TURKEY WITH CHUNKY HONEY-MUSTARD SAUCE

SERVES: 4
WORKING TIME: 25 MINUTES
TOTAL TIME: 25 MINUTES

We don't know who first thought of mixing honey with mustard, but millions of happy eaters have since enjoyed the combination. We've sharpened the hot-sweet contrast (and given the dish a South-of-the-Border slant) by rubbing the turkey cutlets with chili powder and lime juice. Roasted or oven-fried potatoes would be a tasty accompaniment.

1 tablespoon fresh lime juice
1½ teaspoons chili powder
4 thinly sliced turkey cutlets (about 1 pound total)
2 tablespoons flour
½ teaspoon salt
¼ teaspoon freshly ground black pepper
4 teaspoons olive oil
1 red bell pepper, cut into ½-inch squares
3 scallions, thinly sliced
1 cup frozen corn kernels
⅔ cup reduced-sodium chicken broth, defatted
1 tablespoon honey
1 tablespoon Dijon mustard
2 teaspoons cornstarch mixed with 1 tablespoon water

1. In a small bowl, combine the lime juice and chili powder. Brush the mixture over both sides of the turkey cutlets. On a sheet of waxed paper, combine the flour, salt, and black pepper. Dredge the turkey in the flour mixture, shaking off the excess. In a large non-stick skillet, heat 1 tablespoon of the oil until hot but not smoking over medium heat. Add the turkey and cook until golden brown and just cooked through, about 1 minute per side. With a slotted spoon, transfer the turkey to a plate.

2. Add the remaining 1 teaspoon oil, the bell pepper, and scallions to the skillet and cook, stirring, until crisp-tender, about 4 minutes. Stir in the corn and cook until heated through, about 1 minute.

3. In a small bowl, combine the broth, honey, and mustard. Add the mixture to the pan and bring to a boil. Stir in the cornstarch mixture, return to a boil, and cook, stirring, until slightly thickened, about 1 minute. Reduce to a simmer, return the turkey to the pan, and cook until just heated through, about 1 minute. Divide the turkey among 4 plates, spoon the sauce over, and serve.

Helpful hint: If your market doesn't offer thinly sliced turkey cutlets, pound regular cutlets yourself. Place the cutlets between two sheets of waxed paper and using the flat side of small skillet or a meat pounder, pound the cutlets to a ¼-inch thickness.

FAT: 6G/21%
CALORIES: 257
SATURATED FAT: 0.9G
CARBOHYDRATE: 20G
PROTEIN: 31G
CHOLESTEROL: 70MG
SODIUM: 540MG

It
would be a shame to
take sweet, tender
summer vegetables like
sugar snap peas, yellow
squash, and tomato
and then cook them
until their delicate
flavors and ethereal
textures are gone.
Speedy stir-frying is
one of the best ways to
preserve the singular
qualities of vegetables.
Here, the addition of
broth turns this
chicken stir-fry into a
delicious pasta sauce.

SUMMER CHICKEN STIR-FRY

SERVES: 4
WORKING TIME: 30 MINUTES
TOTAL TIME: 30 MINUTES

8 ounces linguine

2 tablespoons plus 2 teaspoons
cornstarch

¾ teaspoon salt

¼ teaspoon freshly ground black
pepper

¾ pound skinless, boneless
chicken thighs, cut into ½-inch
chunks

1 tablespoon olive oil

2 yellow summer squash, halved
lengthwise and thinly sliced

1 tomato, coarsely chopped

1 cup reduced-sodium chicken
broth, defatted

½ pound sugar snap peas, strings
removed (see tip)

⅓ cup chopped fresh mint

1. In a large pot of boiling water, cook the linguine until just tender. Drain well.

2. Meanwhile, in a sturdy plastic bag, combine 2 tablespoons of the cornstarch, ¼ teaspoon of the salt, and the pepper. Add the chicken to the bag, shaking to coat with the cornstarch mixture. In a large nonstick skillet or wok, heat the oil until hot but not smoking over medium heat. Add the chicken and stir-fry until golden brown and cooked through, about 3 minutes. With a slotted spoon, transfer the chicken to a plate.

3. Add the squash to the pan and stir-fry until crisp-tender, about 3 minutes. Stir in the tomato, broth, sugar snap peas, mint, and the remaining ½ teaspoon salt and bring to a boil. Reduce to a simmer and cook until the vegetables are just tender, about 2 minutes. Return the chicken to the pan and cook just until heated through, about 1 minute.

4. In a small bowl, combine the remaining 2 teaspoons cornstarch with 1 tablespoon of water and add the mixture to the pan. Cook, stirring, until slightly thickened, about 1 minute. Serve the chicken and vegetables over the linguine.

Helpful hint: If sugar snap peas are not available (their season is quite short), you can use fresh or frozen snow peas.

FAT: 8G/17%
CALORIES: 421
SATURATED FAT: 1.5G
CARBOHYDRATE: 59G
PROTEIN: 28G
CHOLESTEROL: 71MG
SODIUM: 714MG

TIP

To string sugar snap peas, pinch off the stem and pull the string from the front of the pod. If the sugar snaps are on the large side (making the strings tougher), you may want to pull the string from the back side of the pod as well.

STIR-FRIED CHICKEN AND CASHEWS

SERVES: 4
WORKING TIME: 25 MINUTES
TOTAL TIME: 40 MINUTES

You should think twice before ordering "chicken with cashews" in a Chinese restaurant if you're concerned about fat. The cashews, which are naturally high in fat, may be fried not once but twice. Stir-fry this classic dish at home instead, using skinless chicken breasts, just one tablespoon of oil, and nuts that have been toasted, not fried, for deep flavor.

2 tablespoons reduced-sodium soy sauce

2 tablespoons dry sherry

1 tablespoon cornstarch

2 cloves garlic, finely chopped

1 teaspoon sugar

½ teaspoon ground ginger

½ teaspoon salt

1 pound skinless, boneless chicken breasts, cut crosswise into ½-inch-wide strips

1 cup long-grain rice

1 tablespoon vegetable oil

1 red bell pepper, cut into 1-inch squares

½ cup canned sliced water chestnuts, drained

4 scallions, thinly sliced

⅔ cup reduced-sodium chicken broth, defatted

½ pound snow peas, trimmed and halved crosswise

¼ cup coarsely chopped toasted cashews

1. In a medium bowl, combine the soy sauce, sherry, cornstarch, garlic, sugar, ginger, and ¼ teaspoon of the salt. Add the chicken, stirring to coat. Marinate for at least 30 minutes at room temperature or up to 12 hours in the refrigerator.

2. In a medium saucepan, bring 2¼ cups of water to a boil. Add the rice and the remaining ¼ teaspoon salt, reduce to a simmer, cover, and cook until the rice is tender, about 17 minutes.

3. Meanwhile, in a large nonstick skillet or wok, heat the oil until hot but not smoking over medium heat. Add the bell pepper and stir-fry until crisp-tender, about 3 minutes. Reserving the marinade, add the chicken to the pan along with the water chestnuts and scallions and stir-fry until the chicken is just cooked through, about 3 minutes.

4. Add the broth and the reserved marinade and bring to a boil, stirring, until the sauce is slightly thickened, about 1 minute. Stir in the snow peas and cashews and cook until the snow peas are crisp-tender, about 1 minute. Serve with the rice.

Helpful hints: You can substitute the same amount of dry white wine for the sherry, if you like. To toast the cashews, place them in a small, heavy ungreased skillet and cook over medium heat, stirring and shaking the pan frequently, until golden brown, about 3 minutes.

FAT: 9G/18%
CALORIES: 452
SATURATED FAT: 1.7G
CARBOHYDRATE: 54G
PROTEIN: 34G
CHOLESTEROL: 66MG
SODIUM: 767MG

15

Hot and Sour Chicken Stir-Fry

SERVES: 4
WORKING TIME: 30 MINUTES
TOTAL TIME: 30 MINUTES

Szechuan hot and sour soup gets its fire from freshly ground pepper, and its tart bite from rice vinegar. In this main-dish interpretation, we've turned to slightly different seasonings— hot pepper sauce and cider vinegar—for the predominant flavors.

We've kept the traditional mushrooms and sesame oil, but the tomatoes, which help to meld the tangy sauce, are an innovative addition.

1 cup long-grain rice
¾ teaspoon salt
1 tablespoon dark Oriental sesame oil
1 pound skinless, boneless chicken breasts, cut crosswise into ½-inch-wide strips
3 scallions, cut into 1-inch lengths
2 cloves garlic, finely chopped
1 tablespoon minced fresh ginger
½ pound mushrooms, quartered
1 cup no-salt-added canned tomatoes, chopped and drained
2 tablespoons cider vinegar
½ teaspoon hot pepper sauce
½ teaspoon cornstarch mixed with 1 tablespoon water

1. In a medium saucepan, bring 2¼ cups of water to a boil. Add the rice and ¼ teaspoon of the salt, reduce to a simmer, cover, and cook until the rice is tender, about 17 minutes.

2. Meanwhile, in a large nonstick skillet or wok, heat the sesame oil until hot but not smoking over medium heat. Add the chicken and stir-fry until just cooked through, about 4 minutes. With a slotted spoon, transfer the chicken to a plate.

3. Add the scallions, garlic, and ginger to the pan and stir-fry until softened, about 2 minutes. Add the mushrooms and stir-fry until firm-tender, about 5 minutes. Stir in the tomatoes, vinegar, hot pepper sauce, and the remaining ½ teaspoon salt and cook until slightly reduced, about 2 minutes. Bring to a boil, add the cornstarch mixture, and cook, stirring, until slightly thickened, about 1 minute. Return the chicken to the pan and cook just until warmed through. Divide the rice among 4 plates, spoon the chicken mixture alongside, and serve.

Helpful hint: Ginger keeps well in the freezer (double-wrap it in plastic wrap and foil). You don't have to thaw it before mincing it, and if the skin is very thin you don't even have to peel the ginger.

FAT: 6G/15%
CALORIES: 359
SATURATED FAT: 1G
CARBOHYDRATE: 45G
PROTEIN: 32G
CHOLESTEROL: 66MG
SODIUM: 515MG

GREEK-STYLE CHICKEN WITH GARLIC AND OREGANO

SERVES: 4
WORKING TIME: 35 MINUTES
TOTAL TIME: 35 MINUTES

2 tablespoons flour

½ teaspoon salt

¼ teaspoon freshly ground black pepper

4 skinless, boneless chicken breast halves (about 1 pound total)

1 tablespoon olive oil

5 cloves garlic, finely chopped

¾ cup reduced-sodium chicken broth, defatted

3 tablespoons fresh lemon juice

¾ teaspoon dried oregano

⅛ teaspoon cinnamon

2½ cups cherry tomatoes, halved

1½ teaspoons cornstarch mixed with 1 tablespoon water

1. On a sheet of waxed paper, combine the flour, ¼ teaspoon of the salt, and the pepper. Dredge the chicken in the flour mixture, shaking off the excess.

2. In a large nonstick skillet, heat the oil until hot but not smoking over medium heat. Add the chicken and cook until golden brown and cooked through, about 5 minutes per side. With a slotted spoon, transfer the chicken to a plate.

3. Add the garlic to the pan and cook, stirring, for 30 seconds. Add the broth, lemon juice, oregano, cinnamon, and the remaining ¼ teaspoon salt and cook, stirring occasionally, until slightly reduced and flavorful, about 2 minutes. Add the tomatoes and cook, stirring occasionally, until softened, about 4 minutes. Bring to a boil, add the cornstarch mixture, and cook, stirring, until slightly thickened, about 1 minute. Return the chicken to the pan and cook just until warmed through, about 1 minute. Divide the chicken among 4 plates, spoon the sauce over, and serve.

Helpful hint: If you read the labels carefully, you'll find that two types of oregano are packaged by herb and spice purveyors. Oregano imported from the Mediterranean region is milder than that grown in Mexico. Mediterranean oregano is better suited for use in milder dishes, while the stronger Mexican type works best in chilis and spicy dishes.

FAT: 5G/23%
CALORIES: 199
SATURATED FAT: 0.9G
CARBOHYDRATE: 10G
PROTEIN: 28G
CHOLESTEROL: 66MG
SODIUM: 475MG

The word "oregano" is derived from the Greek words for "joy of the mountains," as this herb grows wild throughout Greece. Oregano often flavors Greek-style chicken dishes; here, we've used it in a saucy sauté along with cinnamon, lemon, and other favorite Greek seasonings. Steamed green beans and a simple salad are all the accompaniment this meal requires.

THAI-STYLE CHICKEN AND VEGETABLES

SERVES: 4
WORKING TIME: 25 MINUTES
TOTAL TIME: 25 MINUTES

A finishing flourish of fresh herbs is typically Thai. Here, basil and mint are the last ingredients added to a colorful stir-fry of chicken, squash, and red bell pepper. Garlic, scallions, soy sauce, and chili sauce supply the dish with savory depth; the herbs, along with some just-squeezed lime juice, provide a tantalizing, bright note.

2 tablespoons plus 2 teaspoons cornstarch

¼ teaspoon salt

1 pound skinless, boneless chicken breasts, cut into 1-inch chunks

1 tablespoon olive oil

3 cloves garlic, finely chopped

4 scallions, thinly sliced

1 red bell pepper, cut into 1-inch squares

2 yellow summer squash, halved lengthwise and cut crosswise into ¼-inch-wide slices

¼ cup fresh lime juice

¼ cup chili sauce

2 tablespoons reduced-sodium soy sauce

¾ teaspoon firmly packed brown sugar

⅓ cup chopped fresh basil

¼ cup chopped fresh mint

1. In a sturdy plastic bag, combine 2 tablespoons of the cornstarch and the salt. Add the chicken to the bag, shaking to coat with the cornstarch mixture.

2. In a large nonstick skillet or wok, heat the oil until hot but not smoking over medium heat. Add the chicken and stir-fry until golden brown and just cooked through, about 3 minutes. With a slotted spoon, transfer the chicken to a plate.

3. Add the garlic and scallions to the pan and stir-fry just until fragrant, about 1 minute. Add the bell pepper and stir-fry for 2 minutes. Add the squash and stir-fry until the bell pepper and squash are crisp-tender, about 2 minutes.

4. In a small bowl, combine the lime juice, chili sauce, soy sauce, brown sugar, and the remaining 2 teaspoons cornstarch. Stir the mixture into the skillet and bring to a boil. Return the chicken to the skillet and stir in the basil and mint. Cook, stirring, just until heated through, about 1 minute.

Helpful hint: Coating the chicken (and thickening the sauce) with cornstarch rather than flour gives the sauce a delicate, translucent consistency. Cornstarch is often used for this purpose in Asian cooking.

FAT: 5G/19%
CALORIES: 239
SATURATED FAT: 0.9G
CARBOHYDRATE: 20G
PROTEIN: 29G
CHOLESTEROL: 66MG
SODIUM: 743MG

STIR-FRIED CHICKEN AND MANGO

SERVES: 4
WORKING TIME: 35 MINUTES
TOTAL TIME: 35 MINUTES

Quick stir-frying here brings out the sweet goodness of mango; chili sauce, ginger, and lime make a superb flavor complement.

⅔ cup long-grain rice

¾ teaspoon salt

2 teaspoons olive oil

2 cloves garlic, finely chopped

1 red onion, halved and thinly sliced

1 pound skinless, boneless chicken breasts, cut crosswise into ½-inch-wide strips

⅔ cup reduced-sodium chicken broth, defatted

⅓ cup chili sauce

¼ cup fresh lime juice

½ teaspoon ground ginger

1½ teaspoons cornstarch mixed with 1 tablespoon water

1 mango, peeled and cut into 1-inch chunks

3 tablespoons coarsely chopped unsalted peanuts

1. In a medium saucepan, bring 1½ cups of water to a boil. Add the rice and ¼ teaspoon of the salt, reduce to a simmer, cover, and cook until the rice is tender, about 17 minutes.

2. Meanwhile, in a large nonstick skillet or wok, heat the oil until hot but not smoking over medium heat. Add the garlic and onion and stir-fry until the onion is crisp-tender, about 3 minutes. Add the chicken and stir-fry until lightly browned, about 4 minutes.

3. Stir the broth, chili sauce, lime juice, ginger, and the remaining ½ teaspoon salt into the pan and bring to a boil. Add the cornstarch mixture and cook, stirring, until slightly thickened, about 1 minute. Add the mango and cook just until the chicken is cooked through, about 1 minute. Divide the rice among 4 plates, spoon the chicken mixture over, sprinkle with the peanuts, and serve.

Helpful hint: The chili sauce used here is not an exotic ingredient—it's the familiar spicy, tomato-based condiment sold in bottles next to the ketchup at the supermarket.

FAT: 8G/19%
CALORIES: 386
SATURATED FAT: 1.2G
CARBOHYDRATE: 48G
PROTEIN: 32G
CHOLESTEROL: 66MG
SODIUM: 903MG

TURKEY AND CHEESE STIR-FRY

SERVES: 4
WORKING TIME: 35 MINUTES
TOTAL TIME: 35 MINUTES

½ cup sun-dried tomatoes (not packed in oil)

1 cup boiling water

8 ounces wide egg noodles

1 tablespoon olive oil

1 pound turkey cutlets, cut crosswise into ½-inch-wide strips

½ teaspoon dried marjoram

¼ teaspoon salt

1 cup frozen peas

⅔ cup evaporated skimmed milk

1 teaspoon cornstarch mixed with 1 tablespoon water

3 ounces goat cheese or feta cheese, crumbled

1. In a small bowl, combine the sun-dried tomatoes and boiling water. Let stand until the tomatoes have softened, about 15 minutes. Drain, reserving the liquid, and coarsely chop the tomatoes.

2. Meanwhile, in a large pot of boiling water, cook the noodles until just tender. Drain well.

3. In a large nonstick skillet or wok, heat the oil until hot but not smoking over medium heat. Add the turkey, marjoram, and salt and stir-fry just until the turkey is no longer pink, about 3 minutes.

4. Add the sun-dried tomatoes and the peas and stir-fry until heated through, about 1 minute. Stir in the evaporated milk and the reserved tomato soaking liquid and bring to a boil. Add the cornstarch mixture and cook, stirring, until slightly thickened, about 1 minute. Sprinkle the goat cheese into the sauce and stir to combine. Divide the noodles among 4 plates, spoon the turkey mixture over, and serve.

Helpful hint: Among the milder goat cheeses are log-shaped Bûcheron and Montrachet. Bûcheron (the name means "large log") comes in 4-pound cylinders and is sold by the slice. Montrachet comes in slender 11-ounce logs.

FAT: 13G/22%
CALORIES: 541
SATURATED FAT: 5.6G
CARBOHYDRATE: 57G
PROTEIN: 48G
CHOLESTEROL: 143MG
SODIUM: 412MG

Try this family-pleasing turkey and cheese dish as a welcome change from tuna-noodle casserole.

MEXICAN CHICKEN AND BLACK BEAN STIR-FRY

While Mexican dishes that contain both chicken and beans are usually slow-simmered (think of chili), this satisfying combination of ingredients works equally well in a stir-fry. Bell peppers and corn round out the dish, and bottled salsa helps you make a delicious Mexican-style sauce in minutes. Serve a tossed green salad on the side.

1 tablespoon flour

1 tablespoon cornmeal

½ teaspoon dried oregano

¼ teaspoon freshly ground black pepper

9 ounces skinless, boneless chicken thighs, cut crosswise into ½-inch-wide strips

1 tablespoon olive oil

3 cloves garlic, finely chopped

1 green bell pepper, cut into ½-inch-wide strips

1 red bell pepper, cut into ½-inch-wide strips

1½ cups frozen corn kernels

15-ounce can black beans, rinsed and drained

1 cup prepared chunky tomato salsa

1 tomato, coarsely chopped

½ cup chopped fresh cilantro or parsley

1. In a sturdy plastic bag, combine the flour, cornmeal, oregano, and black pepper. Add the chicken to the bag, shaking to coat with the flour mixture.

2. In a large nonstick skillet or wok, heat the oil until hot but not smoking over medium heat. Add the chicken and stir-fry until lightly browned and cooked through, about 4 minutes. With a slotted spoon, transfer the chicken to a plate.

3. Add the garlic and bell peppers to the pan and stir-fry until crisp-tender, about 2 minutes. Stir in the corn and beans and stir-fry until heated through, about 2 minutes. Add the salsa, tomato, and cilantro. Return the chicken to the pan and cook, stirring, until heated through, about 1 minute. Divide the mixture among 4 bowls and serve.

Helpful hint: If your family prefers white meat to dark, make this dish with chicken breasts instead of thighs.

FAT: 7G/23%
CALORIES: 275
SATURATED FAT: 1.2G
CARBOHYDRATE: 34G
PROTEIN: 20G
CHOLESTEROL: 53MG
SODIUM: 873MG

Kick off autumn—or any season—with this warming main dish that includes parsnips, turnip, and carrots. Though they are firm and dense, root vegetables cook quickly when cut into slender strips. Another favorite fall flavor is represented here—by an apple and a splash of cider vinegar. The dominant seasoning is sage, that mainstay of holiday stuffings.

STIR-FRIED TURKEY WITH WINTER VEGETABLES

SERVES: 4
WORKING TIME: 30 MINUTES
TOTAL TIME: 30 MINUTES

1 tablespoon olive oil

1 pound turkey cutlets, cut into ½-inch-wide strips

1 white turnip, peeled and cut into ¼-inch julienne strips (see tip)

2 parsnips, peeled and cut into 2-by-¼-inch julienne strips

2 carrots, cut into 2-by-¼-inch julienne strips

½ teaspoon salt

½ teaspoon dried sage

¼ teaspoon freshly ground black pepper

½ pound mushrooms, thinly sliced

1 Granny Smith apple, quartered, cored, and thinly sliced

¾ cup reduced-sodium chicken broth, defatted

2 tablespoons cider vinegar

2 teaspoons cornstarch mixed with 1 tablespoon water

1. In a large nonstick skillet or wok, heat the oil until hot but not smoking over medium heat. Add the turkey and stir-fry until just cooked through, about 2 minutes. With a slotted spoon, transfer the turkey to a plate.

2. Add the turnip, parsnips, and carrots to the pan. Sprinkle with the the salt, sage, and pepper and stir-fry until the vegetables are lightly browned, about 4 minutes. Add the mushrooms and apple and stir-fry just until heated through, about 1 minute. Pour in the broth and simmer until the vegetables are crisp-tender, about 4 minutes.

3. Add the vinegar to the pan and bring to a boil. Stir in the cornstarch mixture and cook, stirring, until slightly thickened, about 1 minute. Return the turkey to the pan and cook until heated through, about 1 minute.

Helpful hint: If parsnips are sold only by the bunch where you shop, use the extra parsnips as you would carrots: Peel and slice them into soups or stews. Or, boil peeled parsnip chunks until tender, then mash and season as you would white or sweet potatoes.

FAT: 5G/17%
CALORIES: 266
SATURATED FAT: 0.8G
CARBOHYDRATE: 26G
PROTEIN: 31G
CHOLESTEROL: 70MG
SODIUM: 490MG

TIP

To cut a turnip into ¼-inch julienne strips, first peel the turnip and then cut it into ¼-inch-thick slices. Then cut the slices into ¼-inch-wide sticks.

Italian-Style Chicken Sauté

SERVES: 4
WORKING TIME: 35 MINUTES
TOTAL TIME: 35 MINUTES

1 tablespoon olive oil

6 cloves garlic, peeled

½ teaspoon dried rosemary

1 small dried chili pepper, or
¼ teaspoon red pepper flakes

2 tablespoons flour

½ teaspoon salt

¼ teaspoon freshly ground black
pepper

4 skinless, boneless chicken breast
halves (about 1 pound total)

½ cup dry red wine

1 tomato, diced

1 cup reduced-sodium chicken
broth, defatted

2 teaspoons anchovy paste

¼ cup chopped fresh basil

2 teaspoons cornstarch mixed
with 1 tablespoon water

1. In a large nonstick skillet, heat the oil until warm over low heat. Add the garlic, rosemary, and chili pepper and cook, turning the garlic as it colors, until the garlic is golden brown, about 4 minutes. Remove and discard the garlic.

2. On a sheet of waxed paper, combine the flour, ¼ teaspoon of the salt, and the black pepper. Dredge the chicken in the flour mixture, shaking off the excess. Increase the heat under the skillet to medium, add the chicken, and cook until golden brown and cooked through, about 5 minutes per side. With a slotted spoon, transfer the chicken to a plate.

3. Add the wine to the skillet, increase the heat to high, and cook, stirring, until slightly reduced, about 1 minute. Stir in the tomato, broth, anchovy paste, basil, and the remaining ¼ teaspoon salt and bring to a boil. Cook until richly flavored, about 3 minutes. Return to a boil, add the cornstarch mixture, and cook, stirring, until slightly thickened, about 1 minute. Reduce the heat to low, return the chicken to the pan, and simmer just until heated through, about 1 minute. Divide the chicken among 4 plates, spoon the sauce over, and serve.

Helpful hint: Contrary to what you might expect, the anchovy paste added to the sauce introduces a richly savory quality, not a fishy taste. You can leave it out, if you like.

FAT: 5G/20%
CALORIES: 223
SATURATED FAT: 0.9G
CARBOHYDRATE: 9G
PROTEIN: 29G
CHOLESTEROL: 68MG
SODIUM: 624MG

A light and spicy tomato sauce, fragrant with rosemary and basil, transforms these boneless chicken breast halves into an entrée with Italian flair. Made with tomato, dried chili pepper, and red wine, the sauce is worlds away from anything you can buy in a jar. Serve the chicken with sauteéd zucchini crescents and diced red peppers; for a more substantial meal, add some pasta or rice.

CHICKEN, POTATO, AND ASPARAGUS STIR-FRY

SERVES: 4
WORKING TIME: 30 MINUTES
TOTAL TIME: 30 MINUTES

In the spring you'll often see signs in Chinese-restaurant windows boasting of seasonal asparagus specialties. You can have your own asparagus festival at home with this Asian-inspired recipe: The chicken and vegetables are glazed with a delicate sesame-scented sauce. In contrast to most Asian stir-fries, we've included potatoes in the dish instead of serving it with rice.

¾ pound small red potatoes, cut into ½-inch chunks

¾ pound asparagus, tough ends trimmed, cut into 2-inch lengths

4 teaspoons dark Oriental sesame oil

1 pound skinless, boneless chicken breasts, cut crosswise into ½-inch-wide strips

1 cup frozen peas

1 cup reduced-sodium chicken broth, defatted

½ teaspoon salt

½ teaspoon dried oregano

¼ teaspoon freshly ground black pepper

2 teaspoons cornstarch mixed with 1 tablespoon water

1. In a large pot of boiling water, cook the potatoes until almost tender, about 8 minutes. Add the asparagus and cook for 2 minutes to blanch. Drain the potatoes and asparagus well.

2. In a large nonstick skillet or wok, heat 1 tablespoon of the sesame oil until hot but not smoking over medium heat. Add the chicken and stir-fry until lightly browned and almost cooked through, about 3 minutes. Add the potatoes, asparagus, and peas and stir-fry until heated through, about 2 minutes.

3. Add the broth, salt, oregano, and pepper and bring to a boil. Add the cornstarch mixture and cook, stirring, until slightly thickened, about 1 minute. Stir in the remaining 1 teaspoon sesame oil, divide among 4 plates, and serve.

Helpful hint: If your asparagus seems rather fibrous at the stem ends, try peeling the stalks with a vegetable peeler.

FAT: 6G/19%
CALORIES: 287
SATURATED FAT: 1.1G
CARBOHYDRATE: 24G
PROTEIN: 33G
CHOLESTEROL: 66MG
SODIUM: 557MG

STIR-FRIED CHICKEN WITH GRAPES

SERVES: 4
WORKING TIME: 40 MINUTES
TOTAL TIME: 40 MINUTES

The French call dishes garnished with grapes "Véronique." In this chicken-and-vegetable stir-fry, the grapes are not for decoration: Along with tomato and celery, the grapes go into a tangy sherry-based sauce, contributing a fresh, sweet-tart flavor that complements the chicken. Use seedless red grapes instead of green, if you like.

1 cup long-grain rice
¾ teaspoon salt
2 tablespoons flour
¾ teaspoon dried thyme
½ teaspoon freshly ground black pepper
1 pound skinless, boneless chicken breasts, cut crosswise into ½-inch-wide strips
4 teaspoons olive oil
2 ribs celery, sliced diagonally into ½-inch pieces
3 cloves garlic, finely chopped
⅓ cup dry sherry
¼ cup reduced-sodium chicken broth, defatted
2 tablespoons sherry vinegar or balsamic vinegar
1 cup chopped tomato
1½ cups seedless green grapes, halved

1. In a medium saucepan, bring 2¼ cups of water to a boil. Add the rice and ¼ teaspoon of the salt, reduce to a simmer, cover, and cook until the rice is tender, about 17 minutes. Meanwhile, in a sturdy plastic bag, combine the flour, ½ teaspoon of the thyme, ¼ teaspoon of the salt, and ¼ teaspoon of the pepper. Add the chicken to the bag, shaking to coat with the flour mixture. Reserve the excess flour mixture.

2. In a large nonstick skillet or wok, heat 1 tablespoon of the oil until hot but not smoking over medium heat. Add the chicken and stir-fry until lightly browned and cooked through, about 4 minutes. With a slotted spoon, transfer the chicken to a plate. Reduce the heat to low, add the remaining 1 teaspoon oil, the celery, and garlic and stir-fry until the celery is crisp-tender, about 3 minutes. Add the sherry, increase the heat to medium, and cook for 1 minute.

3. Stir in the broth and vinegar. Add the tomato, grapes, and the remaining ¼ teaspoon each thyme, salt, and pepper. Bring to a boil and cook until slightly thickened, about 1 minute. In a small bowl, combine the reserved flour mixture with 1 tablespoon of water. Add the mixture to the pan and cook, stirring, until slightly thickened, about 1 minute. Return the chicken to the pan and cook just until heated through, about 1 minute. Divide the rice among 4 plates, spoon the chicken mixture alongside, and serve.

FAT: 7G/15%
CALORIES: 435
SATURATED FAT: 1.2G
CARBOHYDRATE: 56G
PROTEIN: 31G
CHOLESTEROL: 66MG
SODIUM: 554MG

Moroccan food is especially noted for its blending of savory seasonings— pepper, paprika, turmeric, and cumin—with sweet spices like cinnamon, ginger, nutmeg, and the like. Here, chicken is dredged in a typically Moroccan spice mixture, sautéed, and served with crisp-tender vegetables and hot, steaming couscous.

MOROCCAN SPICED CHICKEN WITH FENNEL

SERVES: 4
WORKING TIME: 30 MINUTES
TOTAL TIME: 35 MINUTES

1 teaspoon paprika

½ teaspoon ground cumin

½ teaspoon ground coriander

½ teaspoon ground ginger

¾ teaspoon salt

¼ teaspoon freshly ground black
pepper

4 skinless, boneless chicken breast
halves (about 1 pound total)

1 tablespoon olive oil

2 cups thinly sliced fennel bulb
(see tip), plus ¼ cup chopped
fennel fronds

1 red onion, cut into 1-inch
chunks

1 cup couscous

2 cups boiling water

¾ cup orange juice

⅓ cup reduced-sodium chicken
broth, defatted

2 teaspoons cornstarch mixed
with 1 tablespoon water

1. In a medium bowl, combine the paprika, cumin, coriander, ginger, ¼ teaspoon of the salt, and the pepper. Add the chicken, turning to coat both sides. In a large nonstick skillet, heat the oil until hot but not smoking over medium heat. Add the chicken and cook until browned and just cooked through, about 5 minutes per side. With a slotted spoon, transfer the chicken to a plate.

2. Add the sliced fennel, onion, and ¼ teaspoon of the salt to the pan and stir-fry until the vegetables are crisp-tender, about 7 minutes.

3. Meanwhile, in a medium bowl, combine the couscous, the remaining ¼ teaspoon salt, and the boiling water. Cover and let stand until tender, about 5 minutes.

4. Add the orange juice and broth to the skillet and bring to a boil. Stir in the cornstarch mixture and cook, stirring, until slightly thickened, about 1 minute. Return the chicken to the pan along with the fennel fronds and cook until the chicken is just heated through, about 2 minutes. Serve with the couscous.

Helpful hint: If you can't get fennel, substitute 2 cups sliced celery and ¼ cup chopped parsley; add ½ teaspoon fennel seeds to the other seasonings in step 1.

TIP

To prepare fresh fennel, cut the stalks from the bulb, reserving the fronds. Trim the root end and any tough outer sections from the bulb, then slice the bulb crosswise.

FAT: 5G/12%
CALORIES: 385
SATURATED FAT: 0.9G
CARBOHYDRATE: 48G
PROTEIN: 34G
CHOLESTEROL: 66MG
SODIUM: 603MG

HAWAIIAN CHICKEN STIR-FRY

SERVES: 4
WORKING TIME: 25 MINUTES
TOTAL TIME: 25 MINUTES

In Hawaii, this flavor-packed stir-fry would be prepared with fresh pineapple, rather than canned. You can use whichever you prefer. The fruit provides a delightful counterpoint to the garlicky, slightly hot chicken; bell peppers give the stir-fry a tasty crunch. All you need to complete this meal is a simple green salad and a basket of crusty rolls.

1 tablespoon olive oil
4 scallions, thinly sliced
2 cloves garlic, finely chopped
1 pound skinless, boneless chicken breasts, cut into 1-inch chunks
¾ teaspoon ground ginger
½ teaspoon salt
⅛ teaspoon cayenne pepper
1 red bell pepper, cut into thin strips
1 green bell pepper, cut into thin strips
20-ounce can juice-packed pineapple chunks, drained, juice reserved
1 tablespoon honey
1 tablespoon red wine vinegar
2 teaspoons cornstarch mixed with 1 tablespoon water

1. In a large nonstick skillet or wok, heat the oil until hot but not smoking over medium heat. Add the scallions and garlic and stir-fry until fragrant, about 1 minute. Add the chicken and sprinkle with the ginger, salt, and cayenne. Stir-fry until the chicken is golden brown, about 3 minutes. Add the bell peppers and stir-fry until the peppers are crisp-tender, about 3 minutes. Stir in the pineapple.

2. In a small bowl, combine ½ cup of the reserved pineapple juice, the honey, and vinegar. Add the juice mixture to the skillet and bring to a boil. Stir in the cornstarch mixture, return to a boil, and cook, stirring, until the sauce is slightly thickened and the chicken is cooked through, about 1 minute. Divide among 4 plates and serve.

Helpful hint: If you'd like to serve this stir-fry with rice, put the water for the rice on to boil before you heat the oil for the stir-fry to be sure it will be ready at serving time.

FAT: 5G/16%
CALORIES: 280
SATURATED FAT: 0.8G
CARBOHYDRATE: 32G
PROTEIN: 28G
CHOLESTEROL: 66MG
SODIUM: 352MG

PAN-FRIED CHICKEN WITH PARMESAN GRAVY

SERVES: 4
WORKING TIME: 30 MINUTES
TOTAL TIME: 40 MINUTES

*T*he method for making the sauce in this dish is standard gravy-making technique: Flour, broth, and milk are stirred into the pan in which the chicken has been cooked. The difference is in the fat content—the skinless chicken breasts have been cooked in just one tablespoon of oil, so you get the flavor of poultry drippings without the fat. Also, the broth is defatted, and the milk is 1%.

8 ounces spaghetti
1 tablespoon olive oil
3 cloves garlic, peeled
½ teaspoon dried sage
¼ teaspoon red pepper flakes
½ teaspoon salt
½ teaspoon freshly ground black pepper
4 skinless, boneless chicken breast halves (about 1 pound total)
2 tablespoons flour
¾ cup reduced-sodium chicken broth, defatted
⅔ cup low-fat (1%) milk
10-ounce package frozen Italian flat green beans, thawed
¼ cup grated Parmesan cheese
1 teaspoon grated lemon zest

1. In a large pot of boiling water, cook the spaghetti until tender. Drain well.

2. Meanwhile, in a large nonstick skillet, heat the oil until just warm over low heat. Add the garlic, sage, and red pepper flakes and cook until the garlic is golden and the oil is fragrant, about 5 minutes. Discard the garlic and increase the heat to medium. Sprinkle the salt and black pepper over the chicken, add the chicken to the skillet, and cook until golden brown and cooked through, about 5 minutes per side. With a slotted spoon, transfer the chicken to a plate.

3. Add the flour to the skillet and cook, stirring, until lightly browned, about 1 minute. Add the broth and milk and cook, stirring, until slightly thickened, about 4 minutes. Stir in the green beans, Parmesan, and lemon zest and cook until the beans are crisp-tender, about 2 minutes. Divide the spaghetti among 4 plates, top with the chicken and gravy, and serve.

Helpful hint: If you can't find broad, flat Italian green beans, substitute regular cut green beans.

FAT: 8G/16%
CALORIES: 455
SATURATED FAT: 2.2G
CARBOHYDRATE: 55G
PROTEIN: 40G
CHOLESTEROL: 71MG
SODIUM: 586MG

CHICKEN FLORENTINE

SERVES: 4
WORKING TIME: 20 MINUTES
TOTAL TIME: 30 MINUTES

In culinary parlance, "Florentine" means that a dish is made with spinach. Serve this flavorful dish with glazed carrots.

2 tablespoons flour

½ teaspoon salt

½ teaspoon freshly ground black pepper

4 skinless, boneless chicken breast halves (about 1 pound total)

1 tablespoon olive oil

4 scallions, thinly sliced

10-ounce package frozen chopped spinach, thawed (but not squeezed dry)

1 teaspoon sugar

1 teaspoon cornstarch

1 cup evaporated skimmed milk

2 tablespoons reduced-fat sour cream

½ teaspoon grated orange zest

⅛ teaspoon nutmeg

1. On a sheet of waxed paper, combine the flour, ¼ teaspoon of the salt, and ¼ teaspoon of the pepper. Dredge the chicken in the flour mixture, shaking off the excess.

2. In a large nonstick skillet, heat the oil until hot but not smoking over medium heat. Add the chicken and cook until golden brown and cooked through, about 5 minutes per side. With a slotted spoon, transfer the chicken to a plate.

3. Add the scallions to the pan and cook, stirring, until softened, about 2 minutes. Add the spinach, sprinkle with the sugar, cover, and cook, stirring occasionally, until the spinach is heated through, about 2 minutes.

4. Place the cornstarch in a small bowl. Whisk in the evaporated milk and sour cream. Add the cornstarch mixture to the pan along with the orange zest, nutmeg, the remaining ¼ teaspoon salt, and remaining ¼ teaspoon pepper. Bring to a boil and cook, stirring, until the spinach is well coated and the sauce is slightly thickened, about 1 minute. Return the chicken to the pan and cook just until heated through, about 1 minute. Spoon the spinach onto 4 serving plates, top with the chicken, and serve.

FAT: 6G/21%
CALORIES: 261
SATURATED FAT: 1.4G
CARBOHYDRATE: 17G
PROTEIN: 34G
CHOLESTEROL: 71MG
SODIUM: 480MG

Pan-Fried Chicken with Pepper-Garlic Sauce

Serves: 4
Working time: 20 minutes
Total time: 30 minutes

6 ounces all-purpose potatoes, peeled and thinly sliced

12 cloves garlic, peeled

¾ teaspoon salt

¾ cup jarred roasted red peppers, rinsed and drained

1 teaspoon chili powder

2 tablespoons flour

¼ teaspoon freshly ground black pepper

4 skinless, boneless chicken breast halves (about 1 pound total)

1 tablespoon olive oil

½ cup reduced-sodium chicken broth, defatted

½ cup evaporated low-fat milk

1 tablespoon no-salt-added tomato paste

½ teaspoon dried rosemary

1. In a medium saucepan of boiling water, cook the potatoes and garlic with ¼ teaspoon of the salt until tender, about 10 minutes. Reserving ¼ cup of the cooking liquid, drain the potatoes and garlic and transfer to a medium bowl. Mash with the reserved cooking liquid until smooth. In a food processor, process the peppers to a smooth purée. Stir the pepper purée and the chili powder into the mashed potatoes; set aside.

2. Meanwhile, on a sheet of waxed paper, combine the flour, ¼ teaspoon of the salt, and the black pepper. Dredge the chicken in the flour mixture, shaking off the excess.

3. In a large nonstick skillet, heat the oil until hot but not smoking over medium heat. Add the chicken and cook until golden brown and cooked through, about 5 minutes per side. With a slotted spoon, transfer the chicken to a plate.

4. Add the broth, evaporated milk, tomato paste, rosemary, and the remaining ¼ teaspoon salt to the skillet and bring to a boil. Add the roasted pepper mixture and cook, stirring occasionally, until slightly thickened, about 3 minutes. Return the chicken to the pan and cook until just heated through, about 1 minute. Divide the chicken among 4 plates, top with the sauce, and serve.

Fat: 6g/21%
Calories: 256
Saturated Fat: 0.8g
Carbohydrate: 19g
Protein: 31g
Cholesterol: 71mg
Sodium: 666mg

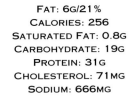

Serve this chicken sauté and its lush (but light) pepper-garlic sauce with steamed Italian green beans.

41

SAUTÉED CHICKEN AND SWEET POTATO "CHIPS"

SERVES: 4
WORKING TIME: 25 MINUTES
TOTAL TIME: 50 MINUTES

½ cup low-fat (1.5%)
buttermilk

1 tablespoon honey

2 tablespoons fresh lime juice

1 teaspoon chili powder

¾ teaspoon salt

¼ teaspoon cayenne pepper

4 skinless, boneless chicken breast
halves (about 1 pound total),
each cut lengthwise into 3 strips

¾ pound sweet potatoes, peeled
and cut into ¼-inch-thick slices

2 tablespoons olive oil

2 teaspoons sugar

¼ cup flour

1. In a medium bowl, combine the buttermilk, honey, lime juice, chili powder, ½ teaspoon of the salt, and the cayenne. Remove ¼ cup of the mixture and set aside. Add the chicken to the mixture remaining in the bowl, stirring to coat. Cover and refrigerate for at least 30 minutes or up to 12 hours.

2. Meanwhile, in a medium pot of boiling water, cook the sweet potatoes for 5 minutes to partially cook. Drain well and pat dry with paper towels. In a large nonstick skillet, heat 1 tablespoon of the oil until hot but not smoking over medium heat. Add the sweet potato slices and sprinkle them with the sugar and the remaining ¼ teaspoon salt. Cook, tossing frequently, until many of the "chips" are browned around the edges, about 5 minutes. Transfer the chips to a plate.

3. Add the remaining 1 tablespoon oil to the pan and heat until hot but not smoking over medium heat. Place the flour on a sheet of waxed paper. Lift the chicken from its marinade and dredge in the flour, shaking off the excess; discard the marinade. Add the chicken to the skillet and cook until golden brown and cooked through, about 4 minutes per side. Divide the chicken and chips among 4 plates and serve with the reserved buttermilk mixture.

Helpful hint: To keep the sweet potato chips warm, place them in a 200° oven while you prepare the rest of the meal.

FAT: 9G/25%
CALORIES: 321
SATURATED FAT: 1.6G
CARBOHYDRATE: 30G
PROTEIN: 29G
CHOLESTEROL: 68MG
SODIUM: 516MG

Sweet potato slices, quickly skillet-browned with a little sugar to glaze them, make nutritious "chips" to accompany sautéed chicken breast strips. The marinade for the chicken is a blend of buttermilk and lime juice, which contributes more than just a sprightly tang: Because it's acidic, it tenderizes the chicken. Serve with a crisp salad and steamed broccoli florets.

SERVES: 4
WORKING TIME: 30 MINUTES
TOTAL TIME: 30 MINUTES

Here's indisputable evidence that a quick, healthful, "from-scratch" meal need not be dull. This stir-fry is packed with bold Mediterranean flavors—garlic, olives, tomatoes, capers, and basil—that transform everyday chicken breasts into something splendid. The stir-fry is served over spinach pasta. Just add some French or Italian rolls and dinner's ready.

6 ounces spinach linguine

1 tablespoon olive oil

1 pound skinless, boneless chicken breasts, cut into 1-inch chunks

1 onion, cut into 1-inch chunks

3 cloves garlic, finely chopped

1¼ cups no-salt-added canned tomatoes, chopped with their juices

⅓ cup raisins

¼ cup green olives, pitted and coarsely chopped

2 tablespoons capers, rinsed and drained

½ teaspoon cornstarch mixed with 1 tablespoon water

1 tablespoon pine nuts

½ cup chopped fresh basil

¼ teaspoon salt

1. In a large pot of boiling water, cook the linguine until just tender. Drain well.

2. Meanwhile, in a large nonstick skillet or wok, heat the oil until hot but not smoking over medium heat. Add the chicken and stir-fry until lightly browned and cooked through, about 5 minutes. With a slotted spoon, transfer the chicken to a plate.

3. Add the onion and garlic to the pan, increase the heat to medium-high, and stir-fry until lightly browned, about 3 minutes. Add the tomatoes, ⅓ cup of water, the raisins, olives, and capers and bring to a boil. Cook until slightly reduced, about 4 minutes. Add the cornstarch mixture and cook, stirring, until slightly thickened, about 1 minute. Stir in the pine nuts, basil, and salt. Return the chicken to the pan and cook until just heated through, about 1 minute. Serve the chicken mixture over the linguine.

Helpful hint: The small amount of spinach used in spinach pasta adds color, but no significant nutrients. The meal will be just as nutritious if you substitute regular pasta.

FAT: 8G/18%
CALORIES: 412
SATURATED FAT: 1.2G
CARBOHYDRATE: 51G
PROTEIN: 35G
CHOLESTEROL: 66MG
SODIUM: 552MG

resh-squeezed lemon juice is a deliciously classic seasoning for asparagus. We've turned this delicate spring vegetable into a substantial main dish here by adding chicken, water chestnuts, and a creamy lemon-dill sauce. If you have a handsome skillet or wok, you can bring this dish directly from the stove to the table.

CHICKEN, ASPARAGUS, AND LEMON CREAM STIR-FRY

SERVES: 4
WORKING TIME: 25 MINUTES
TOTAL TIME: 25 MINUTES

1 pound asparagus, tough ends trimmed (see tip), cut on the diagonal into 2-inch lengths

2 teaspoons olive oil

½ cup finely chopped shallots or scallion whites

1 pound skinless, boneless chicken breasts, cut crosswise into ½-inch-wide strips

½ cup canned sliced water chestnuts, drained

¾ cup reduced-sodium chicken broth, defatted

½ teaspoon grated lemon zest

1 tablespoon fresh lemon juice

1 tablespoon flour

3 tablespoons reduced-fat sour cream

½ teaspoon salt

½ cup snipped fresh dill

1. In a large pot of boiling water, cook the asparagus for 2 minutes to blanch. Drain, rinse under cold water, and drain again.

2. In a large nonstick skillet or wok, heat the oil until hot but not smoking over medium heat. Add the shallots and stir-fry until softened, about 4 minutes. Add the chicken and water chestnuts and stir-fry until the chicken is almost cooked through, about 4 minutes. Stir in the asparagus and stir-fry until just heated through, about 1 minute.

3. In a small jar with a tight-fitting lid, combine the broth, lemon zest, lemon juice, flour, sour cream, and salt and shake until smooth. Add to the skillet and cook, stirring frequently, until slightly thickened, about 2 minutes. Stir in the dill and serve.

Helpful hint: Choose shallots as you do garlic: The cloves should be firm, the skin dry; there should be no green sprouts poking from their tips.

TIP

To prepare asparagus for cooking, hold each spear in your hands and bend it until the stem snaps off; it should break naturally where the woody base merges into the more tender part of the stalk.

FAT: 5G/20%
CALORIES: 225
SATURATED FAT: 1.5G
CARBOHYDRATE: 13G
PROTEIN: 32G
CHOLESTEROL: 70MG
SODIUM: 484MG

STIR-FRIED TURKEY WITH PROSCIUTTO AND BASIL

SERVES: 4
WORKING TIME: 30 MINUTES
TOTAL TIME: 30 MINUTES

The dense, unsmoked Italian ham, prosciutto, is so rich and potent that just a small amount of it imparts a sublime flavor to a skilletful of turkey and vegetables. Fresh basil further emphasizes the Italian theme here. Serve the stir-fry with garlic bread—sliced Italian bread brushed lightly with olive oil, rubbed with a halved garlic clove, and browned under the broiler.

2 tablespoons flour
½ teaspoon salt
½ teaspoon freshly ground black pepper
1 pound turkey cutlets, cut into ½-inch-wide strips
1 tablespoon olive oil
2 ounces prosciutto or Canadian bacon, cut into ¼-inch dice (¼ cup plus 2 tablespoons)
3 cloves garlic, finely chopped
¼ cup fresh lemon juice
⅔ cup reduced-sodium chicken broth, defatted
¾ cup evaporated low-fat milk
1 cup frozen peas
2 teaspoons cornstarch mixed with 1 tablespoon water
⅓ cup chopped fresh basil
⅓ cup chopped fresh parsley

1. In a sturdy plastic bag, combine the flour, ¼ teaspoon of the salt, and ¼ teaspoon of the pepper. Add the turkey, shaking to coat with the flour mixture.

2. In a large nonstick skillet or wok, heat the oil until hot but not smoking over medium heat. Add the prosciutto and cook for 2 minutes to render the fat. Add the turkey and stir-fry until golden brown and just cooked through, about 3 minutes. With a slotted spoon, transfer the turkey to a plate.

3. Add the garlic to the pan and stir-fry until softened, about 1 minute. Stir in the lemon juice and cook for 1 minute to reduce slightly. Stir in the broth, evaporated milk, the remaining ¼ teaspoon salt, and remaining ¼ teaspoon pepper. Bring to a boil and cook for 2 minutes to reduce slightly. Stir in the peas and cook until the peas are heated through, about 2 minutes. Add the cornstarch mixture and cook, stirring, until slightly thickened, about 1 minute. Return the turkey to the pan along with the basil and parsley and cook just until heated through, about 1 minute. Divide the turkey mixture among 4 bowls and serve.

Helpful hint: Canadian bacon, which is smoked, has a different flavor from prosciutto, but it can be substituted, if necessary. Imported prosciutto di Parma is sold in gourmet shops; American versions are sold in most supermarkets, either in packages or at the deli counter.

FAT: 7G/23%
CALORIES: 274
SATURATED FAT: 1.7G
CARBOHYDRATE: 15G
PROTEIN: 37G
CHOLESTEROL: 86MG
SODIUM: 765MG

CHICKEN CREOLE

SERVES: 4
WORKING TIME: 30 MINUTES
TOTAL TIME: 40 MINUTES

2 tablespoons flour

½ teaspoon salt

¼ teaspoon freshly ground black pepper

4 skinless, boneless chicken breast halves (about 1 pound total)

1 tablespoon olive oil

1 onion, diced

3 scallions, thinly sliced

3 cloves garlic, finely chopped

1 jalapeño pepper, finely chopped

1 green bell pepper, cut into ½-inch squares

3 tablespoons dark rum, light rum, or bourbon

1 cup reduced-sodium chicken broth, defatted

2 tablespoons no-salt-added tomato paste

¾ teaspoon ground ginger

½ teaspoon dried thyme

¾ teaspoon curry powder

1. On a sheet of waxed paper, combine the flour, ¼ teaspoon of the salt, and the black pepper. Dredge the chicken in the flour mixture, shaking off the excess.

2. In a large nonstick skillet, heat the oil until hot but not smoking over medium heat. Add the chicken and cook until browned and cooked through, about 5 minutes per side. With a slotted spoon, transfer the chicken to a plate.

3. Add the onion, scallions, garlic, and jalapeño to the pan, and cook, stirring frequently, until the onion is softened, about 5 minutes. Stir in the bell pepper and cook, stirring frequently, until the bell pepper is crisp-tender, about 4 minutes.

4. Add the rum and cook until evaporated, about 1 minute. Stir in the broth, tomato paste, ginger, thyme, curry powder, and the remaining ¼ teaspoon salt. Cook until the sauce is rich and flavorful, about 3 minutes. Return the chicken to the pan and cook just until heated through, about 1 minute.

Helpful hint: The rum or bourbon is optional; you can leave it out if you like.

FAT: 5G/19%
CALORIES: 237
SATURATED FAT: 0.8G
CARBOHYDRATE: 12G
PROTEIN: 29G
CHOLESTEROL: 66MG
SODIUM: 518MG

This is not your usual chicken Creole: Our rendition contains some surprising ingredients—notably a jalapeño pepper, a tot of dark rum, and a spoonful of curry powder. However, these components meld with the traditional onion, garlic, bell pepper, and tomato paste to create an intriguingly complex sauce. Serve some French bread for sopping up every last drop.

TANGERINE CHICKEN

SERVES: 4
WORKING TIME: 35 MINUTES
TOTAL TIME: 35 MINUTES

The pairing of oranges and ginger is featured in some memorable Chinese recipes. We've made this pleasing variation with tangerines, those sweetly perfumed citrus fruits with "zipper" skins. We've boosted the gingery taste by including both minced fresh ginger and ground ginger. Green beans and walnuts also go into the stir-fry, which is served with rice.

⅔ cup long-grain rice
½ teaspoon salt
1 tablespoon vegetable oil
6 scallions, thinly sliced
2 cloves garlic, finely chopped
1 tablespoon minced fresh ginger
2 teaspoons slivered tangerine zest
6 ounces green beans, cut on the diagonal into 2-inch lengths
1 pound skinless, boneless chicken breasts, cut into 1-inch chunks
½ cup fresh tangerine juice
2 teaspoons cornstarch
2 tablespoons reduced-sodium soy sauce
2 tablespoons sherry
1 teaspoon firmly packed light brown sugar
½ teaspoon ground ginger
1 tablespoon chopped fresh parsley (optional)
2 tablespoons coarsely chopped walnuts

1. In a medium saucepan, bring 1½ cups of water to a boil. Add the rice and ¼ teaspoon of the salt, reduce to a simmer, cover, and cook until tender, about 17 minutes.

2. Meanwhile, in a large nonstick skillet or wok, heat the oil until hot but not smoking over medium heat. Add the scallions, garlic, fresh ginger, and tangerine zest and stir-fry until the scallions are softened, about 2 minutes. Add the green beans and stir-fry until the beans are slightly browned, about 4 minutes. Add the chicken and stir-fry until the chicken is just cooked through, about 4 minutes.

3. In a small bowl, combine the tangerine juice and cornstarch, stirring until well combined. Stir in the soy sauce, sherry, brown sugar, ground ginger, and the remaining ¼ teaspoon salt. Add the mixture to the skillet and bring to a boil. Cook, stirring constantly, until slightly thickened, about 1 minute. Divide the rice among 4 plates and sprinkle with the parsley. Spoon the chicken mixture alongside, sprinkle with the walnuts, and serve.

Helpful hints: If tangerines are not available, you can use fresh orange juice, if you like. A twisted tangerine (or orange) slice is an attractive garnish for this dish.

FAT: 8G/20%
CALORIES: 357
SATURATED FAT: 1.1G
CARBOHYDRATE: 38G
PROTEIN: 31G
CHOLESTEROL: 66MG
SODIUM: 658MG

Sautéed Chicken with Pesto Fettuccine

SERVES: 4
WORKING TIME: 20 MINUTES
TOTAL TIME: 30 MINUTES

U*p* with carbos, down with fat: This pesto is thickened with puréed potatoes rather than copious quantities of oil and cheese.

6 ounces all-purpose potatoes, peeled and thinly sliced

¾ teaspoon salt

3 cloves garlic, peeled

1½ cups packed fresh basil leaves

⅔ cup reduced-sodium chicken broth, defatted

4 teaspoons olive oil

2 tablespoons pine nuts

1 tablespoon balsamic or red wine vinegar

8 ounces fettuccine

½ teaspoon dried rosemary

⅛ teaspoon cayenne pepper

4 skinless, boneless chicken breast halves (about 1 pound total)

2 tablespoons flour

1. In a medium saucepan of boiling water, cook the potatoes with ¼ teaspoon of the salt until the potatoes are firm-tender, about 10 minutes. Add the garlic for the last 2 minutes of cooking time. Drain well. In a food processor, combine the basil, broth, 1 teaspoon of the oil, the pine nuts, vinegar, and ¼ teaspoon of the salt and process to a smooth purée. Add the drained potatoes and garlic and process just until smooth, about 30 seconds.

2. In a large pot of boiling water, cook the fettuccine until just tender. Drain well. In a large bowl, toss the pasta with the basil mixture.

3. Meanwhile, in a small bowl, stir together the rosemary, cayenne, and the remaining ¼ teaspoon salt. Rub the herb mixture into the chicken breasts. On a sheet of waxed paper, dredge the chicken in the flour, shaking off the excess.

4. In a large nonstick skillet, heat the remaining 1 tablespoon oil until hot but not smoking over medium heat. Add the chicken and cook until browned and cooked through, about 5 minutes per side. Divide the fettuccine among 4 plates. Slice the chicken on the diagonal and serve alongside the pasta.

Helpful hint: Save a few sprigs of basil for garnishing the finished dish.

FAT: 9G/29%
CALORIES: 271
SATURATED FAT: 1.3G
CARBOHYDRATE: 19G
PROTEIN: 31G
CHOLESTEROL: 66MG
SODIUM: 601MG

BEEF, PORK & LAMB
2

A julienne of turnip, parsnip, carrot, and leek goes into this unusual stir-fry. Cutting vegetables into julienne strips is a standard technique in both Eastern and Western cuisines; the "matchstick" pieces cook quickly and uniformly. Here, the vegetables, tossed with juicy strips of sirloin steak, are served with couscous, the grain-like North African pasta.

STIR-FRIED BEEF AND ROOT VEGETABLES

SERVES: 4
WORKING TIME: 45 MINUTES
TOTAL TIME: 45 MINUTES

¾ cup couscous

1½ cups boiling water

¾ teaspoon salt

1 tablespoon vegetable oil

½ pound well-trimmed sirloin, cut into 2-by-⅛-inch strips

1 leek, white and light green parts only, or 2 scallions, cut into 2-by-¼-inch julienne strips

2 carrots, cut into 2-by-¼-inch julienne strips (see tip)

2 parsnips, cut into 2-by-¼-inch julienne strips

1 turnip, cut into 2-by-¼-inch julienne strips

13¾-ounce can reduced-sodium chicken broth, defatted

2 tablespoons no-salt-added tomato paste

½ teaspoon dried thyme

¼ teaspoon freshly ground black pepper

¼ cup chopped fresh parsley

1. In a large bowl, combine the couscous, boiling water, and ¼ teaspoon of the salt. Cover and let sit for 5 minutes, or until the liquid has been absorbed. Fluff the couscous with a fork.

2. Meanwhile, in a large nonstick skillet or wok, heat 2 teaspoons of the oil until hot but not smoking over medium-high heat. Add the beef and stir-fry until browned, 3 to 4 minutes. With a slotted spoon, transfer the beef to a plate.

3. Add the remaining 1 teaspoon oil to the skillet. Add the leek, carrots, parsnips, and turnip and stir-fry until the vegetables begin to brown, about 2 minutes. Stir in the broth, tomato paste, thyme, pepper, and the remaining ½ teaspoon salt. Bring to a boil, reduce to a simmer, cover, and cook until the vegetables are tender, 3 to 4 minutes.

4. Return the beef to the skillet. Add the parsley and cook until the beef is heated through, about 1 minute. Divide the couscous among 4 plates, spoon the beef mixture alongside, and serve.

Helpful hint: Rice-shaped orzo or another small pasta, cooked according to the package directions, could be substituted for the couscous.

TIP

To cut a carrot into julienne strips, first cut it crosswise into shorter lengths (2 inches for this recipe), then thinly slice each piece lengthwise. Stack the slices and cut them lengthwise into matchsticks.

FAT: 7G/19%
CALORIES: 334
SATURATED FAT: 1.4G
CARBOHYDRATE: 49G
PROTEIN: 20G
CHOLESTEROL: 35MG
SODIUM: 772MG

BEEF AND BROCCOLI LO MEIN

SERVES: 4
WORKING TIME: 30 MINUTES
TOTAL TIME: 30 MINUTES

For the many and varied dishes that come under the heading of lo mein, Chinese cooks toss freshly cooked egg noodles with a sizzling stir-fry. We've substituted vermicelli (very thin spaghetti) for the Chinese noodles. The stir-fry is a mixture of beef and vegetables in a rich, savory sauce flavored with molasses, rice vinegar, and hot pepper sauce.

12 ounces vermicelli pasta

1 pound broccoli

¾ cup reduced-sodium chicken broth, defatted

3 tablespoons reduced-sodium soy sauce

1 tablespoon rice vinegar

1 tablespoon light molasses

½ teaspoon hot pepper sauce

2 teaspoons olive oil

2 cloves garlic, finely chopped

1 tablespoon chopped fresh ginger

¾ pound well-trimmed sirloin, cut into 2-by-¼-inch strips

3 plum tomatoes, halved, seeded, and cut into ¾-inch cubes

7-ounce jar baby corn, rinsed and drained

1 tablespoon cornstarch mixed with 2 tablespoons water

1. In a large pot of boiling water, cook the pasta until just tender. Drain well.

2. Meanwhile, cut the florets off the broccoli and set aside. Peel the broccoli stems and cut into ¼-inch-thick slices. In a small bowl, combine the broth, soy sauce, vinegar, molasses, and hot pepper sauce.

3. In a large nonstick skillet or wok, heat the oil until hot but not smoking over medium heat. Add the broccoli stems and stir-fry for 1 minute. Add the florets and stir-fry for 2 minutes. Add the garlic, ginger, and beef and stir-fry until the beef is no longer pink, about 1 minute. Add the tomatoes, broth mixture, and baby corn and bring to a boil. Stir in the cornstarch mixture and cook, stirring constantly, until slightly thickened, about 1 minute. Toss with the vermicelli and serve.

Helpful hint: Peeling the broccoli stems eliminates the tough outer layer, so they cook more quickly. It's easiest to do with a swivel-bladed vegetable peeler.

FAT: 8G/14%
CALORIES: 518
SATURATED FAT: 1.8G
CARBOHYDRATE: 78G
PROTEIN: 33G
CHOLESTEROL: 52MG
SODIUM: 673MG

LAMB WITH SPRING VEGETABLES

SERVES: 4
WORKING TIME: 20 MINUTES
TOTAL TIME: 30 MINUTES

We've taken a classic French lamb stew and turned it into an innovative stir-fry with a distinct American twist. The lamb is marinated in steak sauce before being stir-fried, and mint jelly (often served with roast lamb) is stirred into the sauce as a finishing-touch flavoring. There are no potatoes in this stir-fry as there would be in a stew, so the lamb and vegetables are served with orzo.

8 ounces orzo pasta

1 tablespoon steak sauce or Worcestershire sauce

2 tablespoons fresh lemon juice

¾ pound well-trimmed boneless leg of lamb, cut into 1-by-¼-inch strips

2 teaspoons olive oil

3 carrots, thinly sliced

½ pound asparagus, tough ends trimmed, cut on the diagonal into ¾-inch lengths

1 zucchini, quartered lengthwise and cut into ½-inch slices

1 red bell pepper, cut into ¾-inch squares

½ cup reduced-sodium chicken broth, defatted

3 tablespoons mint jelly

1 teaspoon salt

¼ pound snow peas

2 teaspoons cornstarch mixed with 1 tablespoon water

1. In a large pot of boiling water, cook the pasta until just tender. Drain well.

2. Meanwhile, in a medium bowl, combine the steak sauce and lemon juice. Add the lamb, tossing to coat well. Let stand at room temperature for 10 minutes.

3. In a large nonstick skillet or wok, heat 1 teaspoon of the oil until hot but not smoking over medium-high heat. Reserving the marinade, add the lamb and stir-fry until no longer pink, 2 to 3 minutes. With a slotted spoon, transfer the lamb to a plate.

4. Add the remaining 1 teaspoon oil to the skillet. Add the carrots, asparagus, zucchini, and bell pepper and stir-fry until the vegetables are crisp-tender, about 5 minutes. Add the reserved marinade, the broth, mint jelly, and salt. Add the snow peas and bring to a boil. Stir in the cornstarch mixture and cook, stirring, until slightly thickened, about 2 minutes. Return the lamb to the pan and cook until heated through, about 1 minute. Divide the orzo among 4 plates, spoon the lamb mixture alongside, and serve.

Helpful hint: You can substitute sugar snap peas for the snow peas, if you like.

FAT: 7G/14%
CALORIES: 447
SATURATED FAT: 1.9G
CARBOHYDRATE: 67G
PROTEIN: 29G
CHOLESTEROL: 55MG
SODIUM: 778MG

SWEET AND SOUR PORK

SERVES: 4
WORKING TIME: 35 MINUTES
TOTAL TIME: 45 MINUTES

1 cup long-grain rice

¼ teaspoon salt

¾ pound well-trimmed pork loin, cut into ½-inch cubes

3 tablespoons reduced-sodium soy sauce

2 tablespoons dry sherry

1 tablespoon minced fresh ginger

2 cloves garlic, minced

2 tablespoons firmly packed light brown sugar

2 tablespoons ketchup

1 tablespoon red wine vinegar

½ teaspoon hot pepper sauce

15-ounce can juice-packed pineapple chunks, juice reserved

2 teaspoons olive oil

1 red bell pepper, cut into ¾-inch squares

1 green bell pepper, cut into ¾-inch squares

3 scallions, thinly sliced

1 tablespoon cornstarch mixed with 2 tablespoons water

1. In a medium saucepan, bring 2¼ cups of water to a boil. Add the rice and salt, reduce to a simmer, cover, and cook until the rice is tender, about 17 minutes.

2. Meanwhile, in a medium bowl, combine the pork, soy sauce, sherry, ginger, and garlic, tossing to coat the pork. Let stand at room temperature for at least 15 minutes. In a small bowl, combine the brown sugar, ketchup, vinegar, hot pepper sauce, and ⅓ cup of the reserved pineapple juice. Set the sweet and sour sauce aside.

3. In a large nonstick skillet or wok, heat the oil until hot but not smoking over medium-high heat. Add the bell peppers and stir-fry until crisp-tender, about 2 minutes. Reserving the marinade, add the pork to the skillet along with the scallions and stir-fry until the pork is just cooked through, about 3 minutes.

4. Stir the reserved marinade into the sweet and sour sauce and add it to the skillet along with the pineapple chunks. Bring to a boil, stir in the cornstarch mixture, and cook, stirring, until slightly thickened, about 1 minute. Divide the rice among 4 bowls, spoon the pork mixture alongside, and serve.

Helpful hint: The pork can be marinated for up to 3 hours and kept covered in the refrigerator.

FAT: 8G/16%
CALORIES: 450
SATURATED FAT: 2G
CARBOHYDRATE: 70G
PROTEIN: 23G
CHOLESTEROL: 50MG
SODIUM: 744MG

Popular as it is, this all-time favorite was due for some trimming down: When prepared by the traditional method, the pork is deep-fried. We've made the entire dish a stir-fry instead, cutting the oil down to a mere 2 teaspoons. The juicy chunks of pineapple and crunchy bell peppers add bright color as well as lively flavor.

ITALIAN BEEF STIR-FRY WITH ARTICHOKES

SERVES: 4
WORKING TIME: 35 MINUTES
TOTAL TIME: 35 MINUTES

Artichoke hearts, mushrooms, tomatoes, and bell peppers signal the Italian inspiration here, as do the garlic and balsamic vinegar that season the sauce. Fresh artichokes take some time to prepare, so we've used frozen artichoke hearts; they have a lighter, fresher flavor than the canned ones because they're not packed in brine. A salad with cucumbers and radishes would be nice with this dish.

8 ounces ruote (wagon wheel) pasta
1 tablespoon oil
½ pound well-trimmed sirloin, cut into 2-by-⅛-inch strips
1 onion, chopped
1 clove garlic, minced
2 red bell peppers, cut into thin strips
9-ounce package frozen artichoke hearts, thawed and quartered
1 cup sliced mushrooms
13¾-ounce can reduced-sodium chicken broth, defatted
½ teaspoon dried thyme
½ teaspoon dried rosemary
½ teaspoon salt
⅛ teaspoon red pepper flakes
1 teaspoon cornstarch
1 tablespoon balsamic vinegar
3 plum tomatoes, diced
¼ cup chopped fresh parsley

1. In a large pot of boiling water, cook the pasta until just tender. Drain well.

2. Meanwhile, in a large nonstick skillet or wok, heat 2 teaspoons of the oil until hot but not smoking over medium-high heat. Add the beef and stir-fry until browned, 3 to 4 minutes. With a slotted spoon, transfer the beef to a plate.

3. Add the remaining 1 teaspoon oil to the skillet. Add the onion and garlic and stir-fry until the onion begins to soften and brown, about 2 minutes. Add the bell peppers, artichoke hearts, mushrooms, broth, thyme, rosemary, salt, and red pepper flakes. Bring to a boil, reduce to a simmer, and cook until the artichokes and bell peppers are tender, 3 to 4 minutes.

4. In a small bowl, combine the cornstarch with the balsamic vinegar and 1 tablespoon of water. Stir the mixture into the skillet along with the tomatoes and cook, stirring, until slightly thickened, about 1 minute. Return the beef to the pan along with the parsley and cook until heated through, about 1 minute. Toss with the pasta, divide among 4 bowls, and serve.

Helpful hint: An egg slicer—the kind with evenly spaced wires like guitar strings—can be used to slice mushrooms quickly and neatly.

FAT: 7G/16%
CALORIES: 389
SATURATED FAT: 1.5G
CARBOHYDRATE: 57G
PROTEIN: 24G
CHOLESTEROL: 35MG
SODIUM: 615MG

Beef and Mushroom Burgers

Serves: 4
Working time: 20 minutes
Total time: 30 minutes

*F*or these thick, juicy burgers, you chop the beef yourself, adding garlic, shallots, capers, and Worcestershire sauce for robust flavor.

⅔ cup reduced-sodium chicken broth, defatted

3 cups quartered mushrooms

½ cup bulghur (cracked wheat)

1 yellow summer squash, coarsely chopped

3 scallions, finely chopped

3 tablespoons ketchup

1 tablespoon balsamic vinegar

3 tablespoons Worcestershire sauce

¾ pound well-trimmed top round of beef, cut into ¾-inch cubes

1 clove garlic, coarsely chopped

2 shallots or scallion whites, thinly sliced

2 tablespoons capers, rinsed and drained

2 teaspoons olive oil

4 hamburger rolls

1. In a medium saucepan, bring the broth to a boil. Add the mushrooms and cook for 1 minute to blanch. With a slotted spoon, transfer the mushrooms to a food processor. Add the bulghur to the hot broth in the saucepan and set aside, off the heat, until the broth is absorbed, about 15 minutes.

2. Meanwhile, in a small bowl, combine the summer squash, scallions, ketchup, vinegar, and 1 tablespoon of the Worcestershire sauce. Set the relish aside.

3. Add the beef, garlic, shallots, capers, bulghur (drained if necessary), and the remaining 2 tablespoons Worcestershire sauce to the mushrooms in the food processor. With on/off pulses, process until the meat is finely chopped and the other ingredients are well combined. Form the mixture into 4 patties about 3½ inches in diameter (about 1 inch thick).

4. In a large nonstick skillet, heat 1 teaspoon of the oil until hot but not smoking over medium-high heat. Add the burgers and cook for 3 minutes. Add the remaining 1 teaspoon oil, turn the burgers, and cook until medium, about 3 minutes. Place the hamburger rolls on 4 plates, top with the burgers and relish, and serve.

Helpful hint: Try toasted English muffins instead of the hamburger rolls

Fat: 8g/20%
Calories: 366
Saturated Fat: 1.9g
Carbohydrate: 47g
Protein: 28g
Cholesterol: 49mg
Sodium: 769mg

SERVES: 4
WORKING TIME: 35 MINUTES
TOTAL TIME: 35 MINUTES

1½ pounds all-purpose potatoes, peeled and cut into 1-inch cubes

½ cup low-fat (1%) milk

¼ teaspoon salt

1 clove garlic, finely chopped

1½ tablespoons minced fresh rosemary, or 2 teaspoons dried

1 teaspoon dried thyme

3 tablespoons red wine vinegar

2 teaspoons olive oil

1 red onion, halved and sliced

4 cups thinly sliced red cabbage

1 Granny Smith apple, cored and shredded

1 tablespoon firmly packed light brown sugar

½ teaspoon hot pepper sauce

¾ pound reduced-sodium ham, cut into ½-inch cubes

1 tablespoon chopped fresh parsley (optional)

1. In a medium pot of boiling water, cook the potatoes until firm-tender, about 10 minutes. Drain well and mash with the milk and salt.

2. Meanwhile, in a small bowl, combine the garlic, rosemary, thyme, and vinegar.

3. In a large nonstick skillet, heat the oil until hot but not smoking over medium-high heat. Add the onion and cook, stirring, until softened, about 3 minutes. Add the cabbage and the rosemary mixture and cook, stirring, until the cabbage is wilted, about 5 minutes. Stir in the apple, brown sugar, hot pepper sauce, and ham and cook, stirring, until the sugar is melted and the ham is heated through, about 3 minutes.

4. Divide the mashed potatoes among 4 plates and sprinkle with the parsley. Spoon the ham mixture alongside and serve.

Helpful hint: If you like, you can substitute green cabbage for the red.

FAT: 6G/18%
CALORIES: 302
SATURATED FAT: 1.6G
CARBOHYDRATE: 45G
PROTEIN: 20G
CHOLESTEROL: 42MG
SODIUM: 893MG

This colorful dish (based on a traditional German recipe) is perfect to serve on a cold, wintry evening.

PORK CUTLETS WITH PLUM SAUCE

SERVES: 4
WORKING TIME: 25 MINUTES
TOTAL TIME: 25 MINUTES

The Chinese plum sauce sold in cans and jars is made from fruit, chilies, vinegar, and sugar. Our homemade version, which includes sliced fresh plums, plum jam, fresh ginger, and orange juice, is the perfect complement to sautéed pork and sweet potatoes. A green salad with red onions offers a nice contrast to the plums.

1 pound sweet potatoes, peeled and cut crosswise into ¼-inch-thick slices

4 well-trimmed boneless pork loin chops (about 3 ounces each)

1 tablespoon flour

½ teaspoon salt

½ teaspoon dried sage

¼ teaspoon freshly ground black pepper

1 tablespoon olive oil

¾ pound red or black plums, pitted and cut into ½-inch slices

4 scallions, chopped

½ cup reduced-sodium chicken broth, defatted

⅓ cup orange juice

¼ cup plum jam

1 tablespoon minced fresh ginger

1 teaspoon cornstarch mixed with 2 tablespoons water

1. In a large saucepan of boiling water, cook the sweet potatoes until firm-tender, 4 to 5 minutes. Drain well.

2. Meanwhile, place the pork chops between 2 sheets of waxed paper and, with the flat side of a small skillet or meat pounder, pound the pork to a ¼-inch thickness. On another sheet of waxed paper, combine the flour, salt, sage, and pepper. Dredge the pork in the flour mixture, shaking off the excess. In a large nonstick skillet, heat the oil until hot but not smoking over medium-high heat. Add the pork and cook until golden brown on the outside and no longer pink on the inside, about 2 minutes per side. Transfer the pork to a plate.

3. Add the plums, scallions, broth, orange juice, plum jam, and ginger to the skillet and bring to a boil. Reduce to a simmer and cook until the plums are almost tender, 1 to 2 minutes. Add the cornstarch mixture and cook, stirring, until slightly thickened, about 1 minute.

4. Return the pork to the skillet along with the sweet potatoes, turning to coat with the sauce. Cook until heated through, about 1 minute. Divide among 4 plates and serve.

Helpful hint: You can substitute turkey cutlets for the pork cutlets, if you like. In step 2, cook them until they are cooked through, about 1 minute per side, and continue with the recipe.

FAT: 9G/23%
CALORIES: 357
SATURATED FAT: 2.2G
CARBOHYDRATE: 49G
PROTEIN: 21G
CHOLESTEROL: 50MG
SODIUM: 420MG

A

cream sauce flavored with delicate dill, sharp mustard, and tart lemon is typical of Swedish cuisine. Such a sauce might grace anything from cured salmon to a pot roast. We've created a lightened version of a creamy Scandinavian-style sauce by using nonfat yogurt and reduced-fat sour cream, and incorporated it into this beef stir-fry served over noodles.

SWEDISH-STYLE BEEF STIR-FRY

SERVES: 4
WORKING TIME: 35 MINUTES
TOTAL TIME: 35 MINUTES

8 ounces wide egg noodles

1 tablespoon vegetable oil

½ pound well-trimmed sirloin, cut into 2-by-⅛-inch strips

2 cups sliced leeks, white and tender green parts only

2 carrots, thinly sliced

1 cup frozen peas, thawed

1 cup sliced scallions

¾ cup reduced-sodium chicken broth, defatted

½ teaspoon salt

¼ teaspoon freshly ground black pepper

2 teaspoons cornstarch

2 teaspoons Dijon mustard

1 teaspoon grated lemon zest

¼ cup reduced-fat sour cream

¼ cup plain nonfat yogurt

¼ cup snipped fresh dill (see tip)

1. In a large pot of boiling water, cook the noodles until just tender. Drain well.

2. Meanwhile, in a large nonstick skillet or wok, heat 2 teaspoons of the oil until hot but not smoking over medium-high heat. Add the beef and stir-fry until browned, 3 to 4 minutes. With a slotted spoon, transfer the beef to a plate.

3. Add the remaining 1 teaspoon oil to the skillet. Add the leeks and carrots and stir-fry until the vegetables are beginning to brown, about 2 minutes. Add the peas, scallions, broth, salt, and pepper. Bring to a boil, reduce to a simmer, and cook until the carrots are tender, 3 to 4 minutes.

4. In a small bowl, combine the cornstarch, 2 tablespoons of water, the mustard, lemon zest, sour cream, and yogurt. Add to the skillet and cook, stirring constantly, until the mixture is slightly thickened, about 1 minute. Return the beef to the skillet along with the dill and cook until heated through, about 1 minute. Combine with the noodles and serve.

Helpful hint: You can substitute an additional 1 cup sliced scallions for the leeks, if you like. Add them with the other scallions in step 3.

FAT: 11G/22%
CALORIES: 449
SATURATED FAT: 2.9G
CARBOHYDRATE: 62G
PROTEIN: 26G
CHOLESTEROL: 94MG
SODIUM: 587MG

TIP

After rinsing and drying fresh dill, use kitchen shears to snip the feathery fronds directly into a measuring cup, avoiding the stems, until you have the amount the recipe calls for.

STIR-FRIED PORK WITH SESAME GREEN BEANS

SERVES: 4
WORKING TIME: 35 MINUTES
TOTAL TIME: 35 MINUTES

The dark, deeply fragrant oil made from roasted sesame seeds is a staple in Asian kitchens. Fortunately, you'll also find it in most supermarkets. Here, sesame oil flavors green beans, summer squash, and scallions as well as stir-fried slices of pork tenderloin. A sprinkling of toasted sesame seeds reinforces the impact of the aromatic oil.

1 cup long-grain rice
¾ teaspoon salt
1 tablespoon flour
¼ teaspoon freshly ground black pepper
½ pound well-trimmed pork tenderloin, cut into very thin slices
2 teaspoons vegetable oil
1 teaspoon dark Oriental sesame oil
½ pound green beans, cut into 2-inch lengths
1 yellow summer squash, halved lengthwise and thinly sliced
1 cup sliced scallions
¾ cup reduced-sodium chicken broth, defatted
1 teaspoon cornstarch
2 tablespoons reduced-sodium soy sauce
1 tablespoon rice vinegar
½ teaspoon sugar
⅛ teaspoon red pepper flakes
2 tablespoons sesame seeds, toasted

1. In a medium saucepan, bring 2¼ cups of water to a boil. Add the rice and ¼ teaspoon of the salt, reduce to a simmer, cover, and cook until the rice is tender, about 17 minutes.

2. Meanwhile, in a sturdy plastic bag, combine the flour, pepper, and the remaining ½ teaspoon salt. Add the pork to the bag, shaking to coat with the flour mixture. In a large nonstick skillet, heat the vegetable oil until hot but not smoking over medium heat. Add the pork and cook until no longer pink in the center, 3 to 4 minutes. Transfer the pork to a plate.

3. Add the sesame oil and green beans to the skillet and cook until the green beans are browned, about 1 minute. Add the squash, scallions, and ½ cup of the broth. Bring to a boil, reduce to a simmer, and cook until the squash is crisp-tender, about 2 minutes.

4. In a small bowl, combine the cornstarch, the remaining ¼ cup broth, the soy sauce, vinegar, sugar, and red pepper flakes. Add the cornstarch mixture to the skillet and cook, stirring, until slightly thickened, about 1 minute. Return the pork to the skillet along with the sesame seeds and cook until heated through, about 1 minute. Divide the rice among 4 plates, spoon the pork alongside, and serve.

Helpful hint: Toast the sesame seeds in a dry skillet over medium heat: Cook, stirring, for 2 to 3 minutes, until the seeds are golden brown.

FAT: 8G/21%
CALORIES: 347
SATURATED FAT: 1.5G
CARBOHYDRATE: 49G
PROTEIN: 19G
CHOLESTEROL: 37MG
SODIUM: 872MG

TEX-MEX STIR-FRY

SERVES: 4
WORKING TIME: 30 MINUTES
TOTAL TIME: 30 MINUTES

A skillet dinner made with strips of sirloin is a cut above the usual ground-beef one-dish meal. And this unique stir-fry, replete with golden corn, bell peppers, chili seasonings, and fresh cilantro, is ready in half an hour, so you could hardly ask for more in the way of convenience. While you're cooking, warm some flour or corn tortillas to serve on the side.

1 tablespoon vegetable oil

½ pound well-trimmed sirloin, cut into 2-by-⅛-inch strips

1 tablespoon chili powder

1 teaspoon ground cumin

⅛ teaspoon cayenne pepper

1 red bell pepper, cut into thin strips

1 green bell pepper, cut into thin strips

1 red onion, sliced

2 ribs celery, sliced

¾ cup reduced-sodium chicken broth, defatted

2 tablespoons ketchup

10-ounce package frozen corn kernels, thawed

1 cup canned red kidney beans, rinsed and drained

1 cup halved cherry tomatoes

¼ cup chopped fresh cilantro or parsley

1. In a large nonstick skillet or wok, heat 2 teaspoons of the oil until hot but not smoking over medium heat. Add the beef and stir-fry until browned, about 3 minutes. Reduce the heat to medium and add the chili powder, cumin, and cayenne. Stir-fry until fragrant, about 1 minute. With a slotted spoon, transfer the beef to a plate.

2. Add the remaining 1 teaspoon oil to the skillet. Add the bell peppers, onion, and celery and stir-fry until the onions are slightly softened, 2 to 3 minutes. Add the broth, ketchup, corn, and beans. Bring to a boil, reduce to a simmer, and cook until the vegetables are tender, 2 to 3 minutes.

3. Increase the heat to high, return the beef to the skillet along with the tomatoes and cilantro, and cook until heated through, about 1 minute.

Helpful hint: To save time later, you can cut up and combine the bell peppers, onion, and celery up to 12 hours in advance and keep them covered in the refrigerator until ready to use.

FAT: 8G/27%
CALORIES: 270
SATURATED FAT: 1.4G
CARBOHYDRATE: 34G
PROTEIN: 20G
CHOLESTEROL: 35MG
SODIUM: 377MG

STIR-FRIED BEEF WITH MUSHROOMS AND PEANUTS

SERVES: 4
WORKING TIME: 35 MINUTES
TOTAL TIME: 35 MINUTES

1 cup long-grain rice

¾ teaspoon salt

1 tablespoon vegetable oil

½ pound well-trimmed top round of beef, cut into 2-by-⅛-inch strips

1 red onion, sliced

2 carrots, thinly sliced

½ pound mushrooms, stemmed and quartered

1 tablespoon minced fresh ginger

1 cup reduced-sodium chicken broth, defatted

2 teaspoons cornstarch

2 tablespoons reduced-sodium soy sauce

1 teaspoon dark Oriental sesame oil

8-ounce can sliced water chestnuts, drained

2 tablespoons coarsely chopped peanuts

1. In a medium saucepan, bring 2¼ cups of water to a boil. Add the rice and ¼ teaspoon of the salt, reduce to a simmer, cover, and cook until the rice is tender, about 17 minutes.

2. Meanwhile, in a large nonstick skillet or wok, heat 2 teaspoons of the oil until hot but not smoking over medium heat. Add the beef and stir-fry until browned, 3 to 4 minutes. With a slotted spoon, transfer the beef to a plate.

3. Add the remaining 1 teaspoon oil to the skillet. Add the onion, carrots, mushrooms, and ginger and stir-fry until the carrots are crisp-tender, 2 to 3 minutes. Stir in ½ cup of the broth, reduce to a simmer, and cook until the vegetables are tender, 2 to 3 minutes.

4. Meanwhile, in a small bowl, combine the cornstarch, soy sauce, sesame oil, the remaining ½ cup broth, and the remaining ½ teaspoon salt. Add the broth mixture to the skillet along with the water chestnuts and peanuts. Cook, stirring, until slightly thickened, about 1 minute. Return the beef to the skillet and cook until heated through, about 1 minute. Divide the rice among 4 plates, top with the beef mixture, and serve.

Helpful hint: For an extra touch of color, sprinkle the finished dish with chopped fresh parsley.

FAT: 9G/21%
CALORIES: 387
SATURATED FAT: 1.7G
CARBOHYDRATE: 55G
PROTEIN: 21G
CHOLESTEROL: 32MG
SODIUM: 929MG

7 6

Variety of texture is a feature of many stir-fries: In this dish, delicately crisp vegetables, tender beef, and smooth sauce are all combined with velvety mushrooms and crunchy water chestnuts and peanuts to provide even more variety than usual. Accompany the main dish with a salad of greens, cucumbers, and tomatoes.

Honeyed Beef Stir-Fry

SERVES: 4
WORKING TIME: 35 MINUTES
TOTAL TIME: 35 MINUTES

Chinese cuisine is often based on the balance of yin and yang, concepts that represent complementary opposites. In cooking, this is expressed in contrasts of hot and cold, crisp and soft, dark and light. The sauce for this stir-fry of sirloin and vegetables is made with equal amounts of lime juice and honey for an appealing balance of sweet and sour.

1 cup long-grain rice
¾ teaspoon salt
1 tablespoon vegetable oil
½ pound well-trimmed sirloin, cut into 2-by-⅛-inch strips
1 tablespoon minced fresh ginger
1 clove garlic, minced
1 red bell pepper, cut into thin strips
½ pound sugar snap peas or snow peas, strings removed
1 zucchini, cut into 2-by-⅛-inch strips
1 cup reduced-sodium chicken broth, defatted
2 teaspoons cornstarch
2 tablespoons reduced-sodium soy sauce
2 tablespoons fresh lime juice
2 tablespoons honey
8-ounce can sliced water chestnuts, drained
2 cups packed watercress, tough stems removed

1. In a medium saucepan, bring 2¼ cups of water to a boil. Add the rice and ¼ teaspoon of the salt, reduce to a simmer, cover, and cook until the rice is tender, about 17 minutes.

2. Meanwhile, in a large nonstick skillet, heat 2 teaspoons of the oil until hot but not smoking over medium-high heat. Add the beef and stir-fry until browned, 3 to 4 minutes. With a slotted spoon, transfer the beef to a plate.

3. Add the remaining 1 teaspoon oil to the skillet. Add the ginger and garlic and stir-fry until fragrant, about 1 minute. Add the bell pepper, sugar snap peas, zucchini, broth, and the remaining ½ teaspoon salt. Cook until the vegetables are crisp-tender, about 2 minutes.

4. In a small bowl, combine the cornstarch, soy sauce, lime juice, and honey. Stir the mixture into the skillet along with the water chestnuts and watercress. Cook, stirring, until the sauce is slightly thickened and the watercress is wilted, about 1 minute. Return the beef to the pan and cook until heated through, about 1 minute. Serve with the rice.

Helpful hint: If the sugar snap peas are on the large side, be sure to pull the strings from both the front and back of the pod as they will both be quite tough.

FAT: 6G/14%
CALORIES: 385
SATURATED FAT: 1.4G
CARBOHYDRATE: 62G
PROTEIN: 20G
CHOLESTEROL: 35MG
SODIUM: 984MG

With its Spanish, French, African, and Native American influences, Louisiana cooking is one of this country's most fascinating regional cuisines. It tends to be quite rich, but thanks to the bold use of herbs and spices, the robust flavors in this beef stir-fry are wonderful on their own, without high-fat enrichments like butter and cream.

LOUISIANA-STYLE BEEF STIR-FRY

SERVES: 4
WORKING TIME: 40 MINUTES
TOTAL TIME: 40 MINUTES

1 cup long-grain rice

¾ teaspoon salt

1 tablespoon flour

½ pound well-trimmed sirloin,
cut into 2-by-⅛-inch strips

1 tablespoon vegetable oil

2 ribs celery, sliced

1 green bell pepper, coarsely
diced

1 onion, coarsely diced

1 clove garlic, minced

1 cup reduced-sodium chicken
broth, defatted

2 tomatoes, coarsely diced

2 tablespoons ketchup

1 teaspoon fennel seeds, crushed
(see tip), or ½ teaspoon ground
fennel

1 teaspoon dried oregano

¼ teaspoon red pepper flakes

10-ounce package frozen sliced
okra, thawed

2 tablespoons chopped green
olives

1 tablespoon chopped fresh
parsley (optional)

1. In a medium saucepan, bring 2¼ cups of water to a boil. Add the rice and ¼ teaspoon of the salt, reduce to a simmer, cover, and cook until the rice is tender, about 17 minutes.

2. Meanwhile, place the flour in a sturdy plastic bag. Add the beef to the bag, shaking to coat with the flour. In a large nonstick skillet or wok, heat 2 teaspoons of the oil until hot but not smoking over medium-high heat. Add the beef and stir-fry until browned, 3 to 4 minutes. With a slotted spoon, transfer the beef to a plate.

3. Add the remaining 1 teaspoon oil to the skillet. Add the celery, bell pepper, onion, and garlic and stir-fry until the onion is beginning to brown, about 2 minutes. Add the broth, tomatoes, ketchup, fennel seeds, oregano, red pepper flakes, and the remaining ½ teaspoon salt. Cook, stirring occasionally, until the vegetables are tender, about 3 minutes.

4. Return the beef to the pan and stir in the okra. Cook until heated through, about 1 minute. Stir in the olives. Divide the rice among 4 plates and sprinkle the parsley over. Spoon the beef alongside the rice and serve.

Helpful hint: Either pitted or stuffed green olives will work well in this recipe.

FAT: 7G/18%
CALORIES: 360
SATURATED FAT: 1.5G
CARBOHYDRATE: 55G
PROTEIN: 19G
CHOLESTEROL: 35MG
SODIUM: 827MG

TIP

Although fennel can be purchased in pre-ground form, its flavor will be more intense if you buy fennel seeds and crush them with a mortar and pestle—the traditional kitchen tool for grinding spices at home. This set is marble; porcelain mortar-and-pestle sets, in a variety of sizes, are also widely available. You can use a mortar and pestle for other whole spices too—cumin, cloves, coriander, anise, and the like.

PEPPER STEAK STIR-FRY

SERVES: 4
WORKING TIME: 30 MINUTES
TOTAL TIME: 30 MINUTES

A trendy restaurant menu might style this dish "four-pepper steak" as it's made with black and white ground pepper as well as red and green bell peppers. An appealing example of "fusion cuisine," this stir-fry is a blend of Asian techniques and Western flavors (the creamy Cognac-mustard sauce is unmistakably French) served with a Middle Eastern pasta.

¾ cup couscous

1½ cups boiling water

¾ teaspoon salt

1 tablespoon flour

¼ teaspoon freshly ground black pepper

¼ teaspoon freshly ground white pepper

½ pound well-trimmed sirloin, cut into 2-by-⅛-inch strips

1 tablespoon vegetable oil

1 red onion, sliced

1 clove garlic, minced

2 red bell peppers, cut into thin strips

1 green bell pepper, cut into thin strips

¾ cup reduced-sodium chicken broth, defatted

1 tablespoon Cognac

2 tablespoons reduced-fat sour cream

1 tablespoon Dijon mustard

1. In a large bowl, combine the couscous, boiling water, and ¼ teaspoon of the salt. Cover and let sit for 5 minutes, or until the liquid has been absorbed. Fluff the couscous with a fork.

2. Meanwhile, in a sturdy plastic bag, combine the flour, black pepper, and white pepper. Add the beef to the bag, shaking to coat with the flour mixture. In a large nonstick skillet or wok, heat 2 teaspoons of the oil over medium-high heat. Add the beef and stir-fry until browned, 3 to 4 minutes. With a slotted spoon, transfer the beef to a plate.

3. Add the remaining 1 teaspoon oil to the skillet. Add the onion and garlic and stir-fry until the onion is just beginning to brown, about 2 minutes. Add the bell peppers, broth, and the remaining ½ teaspoon salt. Bring to a boil, reduce to a simmer, and cook until the bell peppers are tender, about 3 minutes.

4. Stir in the Cognac and cook for 30 seconds. Stir in the sour cream and mustard. Return the beef to the skillet and cook until heated through, about 1 minute. Serve with the couscous.

Helpful hints: Any other type of brandy may be substituted for Cognac, which is the finest (and costliest) of French brandies. You can substitute additional freshly ground black pepper for the white pepper, if you like.

FAT: 7G/21%
CALORIES: 303
SATURATED FAT: 1.8G
CARBOHYDRATE: 37G
PROTEIN: 19G
CHOLESTEROL: 37MG
SODIUM: 669MG

RED FLANNEL HASH

SERVES: 4
WORKING TIME: 30 MINUTES
TOTAL TIME: 30 MINUTES

New Englanders will recognize this time-honored combination of potatoes, beets, and beef; we've used sirloin instead of corned beef.

½ pound red potatoes, cut into ½-inch cubes

2 carrots, cut into ¼-inch dice

1 turnip, peeled and cut into ¼-inch dice

1 parsnip, peeled and cut into ¼-inch dice

1 tablespoon vegetable oil

½ pound well-trimmed sirloin, cut into ½-inch cubes

1 onion, chopped

1 clove garlic, minced

15-ounce can beets, drained and cut into ¼-inch dice

¾ cup reduced-sodium chicken broth, defatted

¼ cup chili sauce

½ teaspoon salt

¼ teaspoon freshly ground black pepper

¼ teaspoon dried thyme

¼ cup chopped fresh parsley

1. In a large pot of boiling water, cook the potatoes, carrots, turnip, and parsnip until firm-tender, 8 to 9 minutes. Drain.

2. Meanwhile, in a large nonstick skillet or wok, heat 2 teaspoons of the oil until hot but not smoking over medium-high heat. Add the beef and stir-fry until browned, 3 to 4 minutes. With a slotted spoon, transfer the beef to a plate.

3. Add the remaining 1 teaspoon oil to the skillet. Add the onion and garlic and stir-fry until the onion begins to soften, 3 to 4 minutes. Add the potatoes, carrots, turnip, and parsnip along with the beets, broth, chili sauce, salt, pepper, and thyme. Cook until all of the vegetables are tender, 2 to 3 minutes.

4. Return the beef to the skillet along with the parsley and cook until heated through, about 1 minute. Divide among 4 bowls and serve.

Helpful hints: Hash is traditionally made with leftovers, so feel free to use leftover cooked carrots or potatoes, should you happen to have some on hand. If you can't get parsnips, you can substitute another carrot, if you like.

FAT: 6G/21%
CALORIES: 256
SATURATED FAT: 1.3G
CARBOHYDRATE: 35G
PROTEIN: 16G
CHOLESTEROL: 35MG
SODIUM: 860MG

STIR-FRIED BEEF WITH TOMATO-PESTO SAUCE

SERVES: 4
WORKING TIME: 40 MINUTES
TOTAL TIME: 40 MINUTES

12 ounces bow-tie pasta

1 cup packed fresh basil leaves

½ cup packed fresh parsley leaves

3 cloves garlic, peeled

2 teaspoons cornstarch

1 cup reduced-sodium chicken broth, defatted

3 tablespoons pine nuts, toasted

1 teaspoon salt

¼ teaspoon hot pepper sauce

1 teaspoon olive oil

¾ pound well-trimmed top round of beef, cut into 2-by-¼-inch strips

2 cups cherry tomatoes, halved

2 tablespoons grated Parmesan cheese

1. In a large pot of boiling water, cook the pasta until just tender. Drain well.

2. Meanwhile, in a food processor or blender, combine the basil, parsley, 1 clove of the garlic, the cornstarch, broth, pine nuts, salt, and hot pepper sauce and process to a smooth purée.

3. In a large nonstick skillet or wok, heat the oil until hot but not smoking over medium heat. Add the beef and stir-fry until still slightly pink in the center. With a slotted spoon, transfer the beef to a plate.

4. Mince the remaining 2 cloves garlic and add them to the skillet along with the tomatoes. Stir-fry for 1 minute and add the basil purée. Bring to simmer, stirring, and cook until heated through and slightly thickened. Return the beef to the pan, stirring to combine. Combine the beef mixture with the pasta. Divide the beef and pasta among 4 bowls, sprinkle with the Parmesan, and serve.

Helpful hint: To toast the pine nuts, place them in a small, dry skillet and cook over medium heat, stirring and shaking the pan, for 3 minutes, or until golden.

FAT: 12G/20%
CALORIES: 532
SATURATED FAT: 2.9G
CARBOHYDRATE: 71G
PROTEIN: 37G
CHOLESTEROL: 131MG
SODIUM: 840MG

This bow tie and beef dish, lightly perfumed with basil, is a nice change from pasta with plain tomato sauce.

CURRIED LAMB WITH COCONUT AND PEPPERS

SERVES: 4
WORKING TIME: 40 MINUTES
TOTAL TIME: 40 MINUTES

1 cup long-grain rice

¾ teaspoon salt

1 pound sweet potatoes, peeled and cut into ¾-inch cubes

2 teaspoons curry powder

2 teaspoons paprika

1 teaspoon ground cumin

¼ teaspoon freshly ground black pepper

2 tablespoons flour

¾ pound well-trimmed boneless leg of lamb, cut into thin strips

2 teaspoons olive oil

1 red bell pepper, cut into thin strips

1 green bell pepper, cut into thin strips

½ cup evaporated low-fat milk

¼ teaspoon coconut extract

2 tablespoons fresh lime juice

1 tablespoon honey

1 banana, cut into ¾-inch cubes

2 tablespoons coconut, toasted

1. In a medium saucepan, bring 2¼ cups of water to a boil. Add the rice and ¼ teaspoon of the salt, reduce to a simmer, cover, and cook until the rice is tender, about 17 minutes.

2. Meanwhile, in a small saucepan of boiling water, cook the sweet potatoes until firm-tender, about 8 minutes. Drain well.

3. In a small bowl, combine the curry powder, paprika, cumin, black pepper, and the remaining ½ teaspoon salt. In a medium bowl, combine the flour with 2 teaspoons of the spice mixture. Add the lamb, tossing to coat. In a large nonstick skillet or wok, heat 1 teaspoon of the oil until hot but not smoking over medium heat. Add the lamb and stir-fry just until browned, about 3 minutes. With a slotted spoon, transfer the lamb to a plate.

4. Add the remaining 1 teaspoon oil to the skillet. Add the bell peppers and stir-fry until softened, about 4 minutes. Add the remaining spice mixture and cook until fragrant, about 1 minute. Add the milk, coconut extract, lime juice, and honey. Return the lamb to the pan, tossing to coat with the sauce, and cook until heated through, about 1 minute. Add the sweet potatoes and banana, tossing gently to combine. Divide the rice among 4 plates. Spoon the lamb mixture alongside, sprinkle with the coconut, and serve.

Helpful hint: To toast the coconut, spread it in a small baking pan and toast in a 350° oven for 8 to 10 minutes, until golden.

FAT: 9G/16%
CALORIES: 499
SATURATED FAT: 2.5G
CARBOHYDRATE: 80G
PROTEIN: 26G
CHOLESTEROL: 60MG
SODIUM: 519MG

Coconut milk—produced by mashing coconut flesh to extract the rich oils—is a staple in Southeast Asian kitchens, bringing sweet, velvety richness to soups, sauces, and curries. But since its fat content runs a close second to heavy cream, we've replaced the coconut milk in this flavorful but light lamb stir-fry with a mixture of evaporated low-fat milk and coconut extract.

PORK CUTLETS WITH CAPERS AND SAGE

SERVES: 4
WORKING TIME: 40 MINUTES
TOTAL TIME: 40 MINUTES

Inspired by veal scaloppine, this substantial main course is centered around pork "scallops"— boneless chops that are pounded thin, dredged in seasoned flour, and then sautéed. The sage-scented mushroom sauce, which is quickly made from the pan juices, also boasts the bright flavors of lemon, capers, and fresh parsley.

8 ounces rotini (fusilli) pasta

4 well-trimmed boneless pork loin chops (about 3 ounces each)

1 tablespoon flour

¼ teaspoon freshly ground black pepper

¾ teaspoon salt

1 tablespoon olive oil

1 onion, thinly sliced

1 clove garlic, minced

1 cup reduced-sodium chicken broth, defatted

2 cups sliced mushrooms

½ teaspoon dried sage

½ cup evaporated skimmed milk

1 teaspoon cornstarch

2 tablespoons capers, rinsed and drained

1 tablespoon fresh lemon juice

¼ cup chopped fresh parsley (optional)

1. In a large pot of boiling water, cook the pasta until just tender. Drain well.

2. Meanwhile, place the pork chops between 2 sheets of waxed paper and with the flat side of a small skillet or meat pounder, pound the pork to a ¼-inch thickness. On another sheet of waxed paper, combine the flour, pepper, and ¼ teaspoon of the salt. Dredge the pork in the flour mixture, shaking off the excess.

3. In a large nonstick skillet, heat 2 teaspoons of the oil until hot but not smoking over medium-high heat. Add the pork and cook until no longer pink in the center, about 2 minutes. Transfer to a plate and cover loosely with foil to keep warm. Add the remaining 1 teaspoon oil to the skillet. Add the onion and garlic and cook, stirring, until the onion begins to brown, 1 to 2 minutes. Add the broth, mushrooms, sage, and the remaining ½ teaspoon salt. Bring to a boil, reduce to a simmer, and cook until the mushrooms are tender, about 2 minutes.

4. Meanwhile, in a small bowl, combine the evaporated milk and cornstarch. Stir the milk mixture into the skillet and cook, stirring, until slightly thickened, about 1 minute. Stir in the capers, lemon juice, and parsley. Serve the sauce over the pork and the pasta.

FAT: 9G/19%
CALORIES: 429
SATURATED FAT: 2.3G
CARBOHYDRATE: 55G
PROTEIN: 30G
CHOLESTEROL: 51MG
SODIUM: 772MG

Sautéed Beef with Salsa Verde Beans

Serves: 4
Working time: 25 minutes
Total time: 35 minutes

This skillet-cooked steak is served with lima beans in a lively lemon-caper sauce. Roasted corn on the cob would be a perfect side dish.

Two 10-ounce packages frozen lima beans

½ cup reduced-sodium chicken broth, defatted

¼ cup fresh lemon juice

1 tablespoon anchovy paste

½ teaspoon salt

8 scallions, finely chopped

½ cup chopped fresh parsley

¼ cup capers, rinsed and drained

1 pound well-trimmed top round steak

1 tablespoon flour

1 teaspoon olive oil

1. In a large saucepan of boiling water, cook the lima beans until tender, about 7 minutes. Drain well. Transfer half of the beans to a food processor or blender. Add the broth, lemon juice, anchovy paste, and salt and process to a smooth purée. Transfer the mixture to a bowl and stir in the scallions, parsley, and capers.

2. With a sharp knife, lightly score the steak at 1-inch intervals. Place the steak between 2 sheets of waxed paper and with the flat side of a small skillet or meat pounder, pound the steak to a ¾-inch thickness. Dredge the steak in the flour, shaking off the excess.

3. In a large nonstick skillet, heat the oil until hot but not smoking over medium heat. Add the steak and cook, turning 2 or 3 times, until medium-rare, about 12 minutes. Transfer the steak to a cutting board and let stand for 10 minutes before thinly slicing on the diagonal.

4. Add the sauce to the skillet, stir in the remaining lima beans, and cook just until heated through. Divide the lima bean mixture among 4 plates and serve the sliced beef alongside.

Helpful hint: Top round, flank, and other lean steaks should be sliced on the diagonal to render the meat as tender as possible.

Fat: 6g/16%
Calories: 339
Saturated Fat: 1.6g
Carbohydrate: 34g
Protein: 38g
Cholesterol: 67mg
Sodium: 888mg

ASIAN-STYLE RED PEPPER AND TOFU STIR-FRY

SERVES: 4
WORKING TIME: 35 MINUTES
TOTAL TIME: 35 MINUTES

Because tofu has only the mildest of flavors, it provides a perfect smooth-textured backdrop for assertive seasonings, such as the vinegar and soy sauce combination in this stir-fry. Vegetarians appreciate tofu as a high-protein meat substitute, while meat eaters find its delicate texture a nice change from beef or chicken.

1 cup long-grain rice

½ teaspoon salt

1 tablespoon vegetable oil

2 red bell peppers, cut into 1-inch squares

3 cloves garlic, finely chopped

1 tablespoon finely chopped fresh ginger

1 teaspoon sugar

3 tablespoons rice vinegar

1 yellow summer squash, halved lengthwise and cut into ¼-inch-thick slices

½ pound sugar snap peas, strings removed

8-ounce can sliced bamboo shoots, drained

8-ounce can sliced water chestnuts, drained

8 ounces firm tofu, cut into ½-inch chunks

½ teaspoon cornstarch

3 tablespoons reduced-sodium soy sauce

⅓ cup chopped fresh cilantro, basil, or parsley

1. In a medium saucepan, bring 2¼ cups of water to a boil. Add the rice and ¼ teaspoon of the salt, reduce to a simmer, cover, and cook until the rice is tender, about 17 minutes.

2. Meanwhile, in a large nonstick skillet or wok, heat the oil until hot but not smoking over medium heat. Add the bell peppers, garlic, and ginger. Sprinkle the sugar and 1 tablespoon of the vinegar over the vegetables and stir-fry until crisp-tender, about 3 minutes.

3. Add the yellow squash, sugar snap peas, bamboo shoots, and water chestnuts to the pan and stir-fry until crisp-tender, about 3 minutes. Add the tofu and stir very gently until just heated through, about 2 minutes.

4. In a small bowl, combine the cornstarch, soy sauce, the remaining 2 tablespoons vinegar, and remaining ¼ teaspoon salt, whisking until well combined. Add 3 tablespoons of water, whisk again, and pour the mixture over the vegetables. Add the cilantro and cook, stirring, until the sauce is slightly thickened, about 1 minute. Serve with the rice.

Helpful hint: You can substitute fresh or frozen snow peas for the sugar snap peas, if you like.

FAT: 9G/22%
CALORIES: 372
SATURATED FAT: 1.3G
CARBOHYDRATE: 59G
PROTEIN: 17G
CHOLESTEROL: 0MG
SODIUM: 802MG

GREEN BEANS, RED BEANS, AND COCONUT CURRY

SERVES: 4
WORKING TIME: 35 MINUTES
TOTAL TIME: 35 MINUTES

We've used green beans and kidney beans in this dish to approximate the hearty quality of Asian green beans, whose flavor and texture combine the crunch of fresh beans with the sturdy starchiness of dried beans. A spicy-hot curry sauce made with evaporated skimmed milk is a creamy complement to the beans and tomatoes.

1 cup long-grain rice

½ teaspoon salt

1 cup evaporated skimmed milk

¼ cup flaked coconut

1¼ teaspoons curry powder

¾ teaspoon ground cumin

½ teaspoon ground ginger

¾ pound green beans, cut into 1-inch lengths

1 tablespoon olive oil

4 scallions, thinly sliced

1 pickled jalapeño pepper, seeded and finely chopped

1½ cups cherry tomatoes, halved

16-ounce can red kidney beans, rinsed and drained

1 teaspoon cornstarch mixed with 1 tablespoon water

2 tablespoons chopped peanuts

1. In a medium saucepan, bring 2¼ cups of water to a boil. Add the rice and ¼ teaspoon of the salt, reduce to a simmer, cover, and cook until the rice is tender, about 17 minutes.

2. Meanwhile, in a blender, combine the evaporated milk, coconut, curry powder, cumin, ginger, and the remaining ¼ teaspoon salt. Process until well combined and slightly pasty, about 1 minute.

3. In a medium saucepan of boiling water, cook the green beans for 2 minutes to blanch. Drain. In a large nonstick skillet or wok, heat the oil until hot but not smoking over medium heat. Add the scallions and jalapeño and stir-fry until the scallions are softened, about 1 minute.

4. Add the green beans and tomatoes to the pan and stir-fry until the beans are heated through and the tomatoes begin to release their juices, about 3 minutes. Add the kidney beans and stir-fry until heated through, about 2 minutes. Pour in the coconut-milk mixture and bring to a boil. Stir in the cornstarch mixture and cook, stirring, until slightly thickened, about 1 minute. Divide the rice among 4 plates. Spoon the vegetable mixture alongside the rice, sprinkle the peanuts over the vegetables, and serve.

Helpful hint: Jalapeños, like all chili peppers, contain volatile oils that can burn the skin—when working with them, wear plastic gloves.

FAT: 9G/19%
CALORIES: 423
SATURATED FAT: 2.3G
CARBOHYDRATE: 70G
PROTEIN: 18G
CHOLESTEROL: 3MG
SODIUM: 569MG

Why settle for plain old potato pancakes? In addition to white potatoes, these crunchy-crusted pancakes include the earthy flavors of parsnips, turnips, sweet potatoes, and onion. The topping is cider-simmered apples and a dollop of yogurt. Enjoy the pancakes as a light meal, or serve half-portions as a side dish to beef or poultry.

Vegetable Pancakes

SERVES: 4
WORKING TIME: 45 MINUTES
TOTAL TIME: 45 MINUTES

10 ounces all-purpose potatoes, peeled

½ pound sweet potatoes, peeled

2 parsnips, peeled

½ pound turnips, peeled

1 medium onion

3 tablespoons flour

¾ teaspoon salt

½ teaspoon dried marjoram

½ teaspoon baking powder

½ teaspoon freshly ground black pepper

1 egg white

2 tablespoons plus 2 teaspoons olive oil

⅔ cup apple cider or apple juice

2 large tart red apples, such as McIntosh, Cortland, or Empire, cut into ¼-inch cubes

1 tablespoon apple cider vinegar

½ cup plain nonfat yogurt

1. On the large holes of a box grater, grate the potatoes, sweet potatoes, parsnips, turnips, and onion into a medium bowl. Stir in the flour, salt, marjoram, baking powder, and ¼ teaspoon of the pepper. Stir in the egg white until well combined.

2. In a large nonstick skillet, heat 4 teaspoons of the oil until hot but not smoking over medium heat. Drop 4 patties of the vegetable mixture by rounded ½ cupfuls onto the pan and flatten to 4-inch rounds (see tip; top photo). Cook until set and browned on the bottom, about 5 minutes. Turn the pancakes over (bottom photo), reduce the heat to low, and cook until browned on the bottom and cooked through, about 5 minutes. Transfer to a platter and cover with foil to keep warm. Repeat with the remaining 4 teaspoons oil and pancake mixture for a total of 8 pancakes.

3. Meanwhile, in a medium saucepan, heat the cider over medium heat. Add the apples, vinegar, and the remaining ¼ teaspoon pepper and cook, stirring frequently, until the apples are crisp-tender, about 5 minutes. Divide the pancakes among 4 plates. Spoon the apple mixture over the pancakes, top with a dollop of yogurt, and serve.

Helpful hints: Carrots can be substituted for the parsnips. If you have a food processor, you can use the shredding blade to grate the vegetables in step 1.

FAT: 10G/26%
CALORIES: 349
SATURATED FAT: 1.4G
CARBOHYDRATE: 62G
PROTEIN: 7G
CHOLESTEROL: 1MG
SODIUM: 556MG

TIP

Drop ½-cup portions of the pancake mixture into the skillet, then flatten them into 4-inch rounds using the bottom of the measuring cup. When the pancakes are browned on the bottoms, carefully turn them and brown the other side.

VEGETABLE STIR-FRY WITH SATAY SAUCE

SERVES: 4
WORKING TIME: 30 MINUTES
TOTAL TIME: 30 MINUTES

8 ounces fettuccine

2 teaspoons vegetable oil

3 scallions, cut into 1-inch lengths

2 cloves garlic, finely chopped

1 tablespoon finely chopped fresh ginger

1 pickled jalapeño pepper, seeded and finely chopped

2 red bell peppers, cut into thin strips

2 large carrots, cut into 2-by-⅛-inch julienne strips

2 turnips, peeled and cut into 2-by-⅛-inch julienne strips

½ teaspoon salt

1 cucumber, peeled, halved lengthwise, seeded, and cut into thin julienne strips

1 teaspoon cornstarch

1½ cups reduced-sodium chicken broth, defatted

¼ cup fresh lime juice

4 tablespoons creamy peanut butter

1 tablespoon firmly packed brown sugar

1. In a large pot of boiling water, cook the fettuccine until just tender. Drain well.

2. Meanwhile, in a large nonstick skillet or wok, heat the oil until hot but not smoking over medium heat. Add the scallions, garlic, ginger, and jalapeño and stir-fry until the scallions are softened, about 2 minutes. Add the bell peppers, carrots, turnips, and salt and stir-fry until the vegetables are crisp-tender, about 5 minutes. Add the cucumber and cook until the cucumbers are heated through, about 2 minutes.

3. In a small bowl, combine the cornstarch, broth, lime juice, peanut butter, and brown sugar, whisking until well combined. Pour the mixture over the vegetables and bring to a boil. Add the pasta and toss to combine. Divide the pasta mixture among 4 plates and serve.

Helpful hint: To seed a cucumber, halve it lengthwise and scoop out the seeds with the tip of a small spoon.

FAT: 13G/28%
CALORIES: 420
SATURATED FAT: 2.2G
CARBOHYDRATE: 63G
PROTEIN: 16G
CHOLESTEROL: 54MG
SODIUM: 721MG

Satays—miniature kebabs that are a popular snack in Southeast Asia—are traditionally served with a spicy peanut dipping sauce that's tasty enough to eat on its own. We've sauced this colorful noodle-and-vegetable stir-fry with a similar peanut-butter-based sauce. Note the use of cucumbers in the stir-fry: They're just heated through so they still retain a touch of crispness.

VEGETABLE HASH

SERVES: 4
WORKING TIME: 30 MINUTES
TOTAL TIME: 40 MINUTES PLUS DRAINING TIME

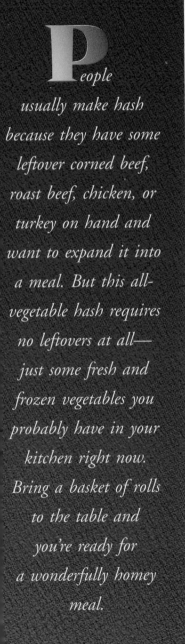

*P*eople usually make hash because they have some leftover corned beef, roast beef, chicken, or turkey on hand and want to expand it into a meal. But this all-vegetable hash requires no leftovers at all— just some fresh and frozen vegetables you probably have in your kitchen right now. Bring a basket of rolls to the table and you're ready for a wonderfully homey meal.

1½ cups plain nonfat yogurt
½ cup chopped fresh parsley
¼ cup chopped fresh mint
¾ teaspoon salt
1 pound small red potatoes, quartered
2 tablespoons olive oil
1 small onion, finely chopped
4 cloves garlic, finely chopped
2 red bell peppers, diced
9-ounce package frozen artichoke hearts, thawed
1 cup frozen peas

1. In a small fine-mesh sieve or a coarse sieve lined with cheesecloth (or paper towels), drain the yogurt in the refrigerator for 1 hour or up to 8 hours. Transfer to a small bowl and stir in ¼ cup of the parsley, 2 tablespoons of the mint, and ¼ teaspoon of the salt.

2. Meanwhile, in a medium saucepan of boiling water, cook the potatoes until tender, about 12 minutes. Drain. In a large nonstick skillet or wok, heat the oil until hot but not smoking over medium heat. Add the onion and garlic and stir-fry until the onion is softened, about 4 minutes. Add the bell peppers and stir-fry until the bell peppers are crisp-tender, about 4 minutes. Stir in the potatoes and artichoke hearts and stir-fry until the potatoes are lightly browned and the artichoke hearts are tender, about 5 minutes.

3. Sprinkle the remaining ¼ cup parsley, remaining 2 tablespoons mint, and remaining ½ teaspoon salt over the vegetables and stir-fry for 1 minute to combine. Add the peas and cook, stirring frequently, until heated through, about 2 minutes. Divide the mixture among 4 plates, spoon the yogurt mixture alongside, and serve.

Helpful hint: You can make the yogurt sauce in advance: Set the yogurt to drain in the evening, then add the herbs and salt in the morning, and refrigerate the sauce in a covered container until serving time. The longer you let the yogurt drain, the thicker the sauce will be.

FAT: 8G/26%
CALORIES: 282
SATURATED FAT: 1.1G
CARBOHYDRATE: 44G
PROTEIN: 12G
CHOLESTEROL: 2MG
SODIUM: 564MG

SCRAMBLED EGGS AND ASPARAGUS

SERVES: 4
WORKING TIME: 30 MINUTES
TOTAL TIME: 30 MINUTES

We've cut five egg yolks (and a lot of fat) from this dish by thickening the egg mixture with cottage cheese and a bit of flour.

1 pound asparagus, tough ends trimmed, cut into 1-inch lengths

¾ pound all-purpose potatoes, peeled and cut into ½-inch cubes

2 teaspoons olive oil

1 onion, coarsely chopped

2 whole eggs

5 egg whites

½ cup low-fat (1%) cottage cheese

3 tablespoons grated Parmesan cheese

2 teaspoons flour

½ teaspoon salt

½ teaspoon dried marjoram

¼ teaspoon freshly ground black pepper

1. In a large pot of boiling water, cook the asparagus for 2 minutes to blanch. Remove with a skimmer or slotted spoon and set aside. Return the water to a boil, add the potatoes, and cook until firm-tender, about 5 minutes. Drain well.

2. In a large nonstick skillet or wok, heat the oil until hot but not smoking over medium heat. Add the potatoes and onion and stir-fry until the onion is softened, about 5 minutes.

3. Meanwhile, in a food processor, combine the whole eggs, egg whites, cottage cheese, Parmesan, flour, salt, marjoram, and pepper and process until smooth. Add the asparagus to the skillet, stirring to coat. Add the egg mixture, reduce the heat to low, and cook, stirring, until the eggs are just set, about 7 minutes. Divide the mixture among 4 plates and serve.

Helpful hint: For a change, season the eggs with thyme, basil, or dill instead of marjoram.

FAT: 7G/29%
CALORIES: 207
SATURATED FAT: 2G
CARBOHYDRATE: 21G
PROTEIN: 17G
CHOLESTEROL: 110MG
SODIUM: 565MG

Felafel Burgers

Serves: 4
Working time: 30 minutes
Total time: 40 minutes

½ pound baking potatoes, peeled and thinly sliced

6 cloves garlic, peeled

16-ounce can chick-peas, rinsed and drained

½ cup chopped fresh cilantro or parsley

¼ cup fresh lemon juice

¾ teaspoon salt

¼ cup flour

½ teaspoon baking powder

1 tablespoon dark Oriental sesame oil

½ cup plain nonfat yogurt

1 tablespoon creamy peanut butter

1 teaspoon paprika

½ teaspoon ground cumin

1 tomato, chopped

1 cucumber, peeled, seeded, and finely chopped

Four 6-inch pita breads

2 cups shredded curly leaf lettuce

1. In a medium pot of boiling water, cook the potatoes and garlic until tender, about 10 minutes. Drain, transfer to a large bowl, add the chick-peas, and mash until well combined but still chunky. Stir in the cilantro, 2 tablespoons of the lemon juice, and ½ teaspoon of the salt. Stir until well combined, then add the flour and the baking powder. Shape into 4 patties about 4 inches in diameter.

2. In a large nonstick skillet, heat the sesame oil until hot but not smoking over medium heat. Add the patties and cook, turning them as they brown, until crisp, browned, and heated through, about 7 minutes.

3. Meanwhile, in a small bowl, stir together the yogurt, peanut butter, paprika, cumin, the remaining 2 tablespoons lemon juice, and remaining ¼ teaspoon salt. Add the tomato and cucumber. Cut off the tops of each pita and open the bread to make a pocket. Fill the pitas with half of the lettuce and half of the yogurt sauce. Place a patty inside each pita, top with the remaining yogurt sauce and lettuce, and serve.

Helpful hint: The peanut butter in the sauce takes the place of tahina (or tahini), the sesame butter widely used in Middle Eastern cooking. Substitute tahina if you wish. Its fat content is almost identical to that of peanut butter.

Fat: 9g/20%
Calories: 407
Saturated Fat: 1.1g
Carbohydrate: 69g
Protein: 15g
Cholesterol: 1mg
Sodium: 973mg

Sautéing (rather than deep-frying) the patties makes this Middle Eastern favorite a tasty, healthy dish.

CURRIED VEGETABLE STIR-FRY

SERVES: 4
WORKING TIME: 25 MINUTES
TOTAL TIME: 35 MINUTES

*S*low braising is the usual method for cooking Indian curries, but a vegetable curry can be prepared in considerably less time than one made with meat. This lovely gold-and-green main dish includes sweet potatoes, cauliflower, chick-peas, and fresh spinach. And for fuller flavor, packaged curry powder is spiked with cumin, coriander, and chili powder.

1 cup long-grain rice

¾ teaspoon salt

1 pound sweet potatoes, peeled and cut into ½-inch chunks

1 tablespoon vegetable oil

3 cups cauliflower florets

4 cloves garlic, finely chopped

1 tablespoon minced fresh ginger

2 tomatoes, diced

1 teaspoon curry powder

1 teaspoon ground cumin

1 teaspoon ground coriander

1 teaspoon chili powder

16-ounce can chick-peas, rinsed and drained

10 ounces fresh spinach, stems removed

2 tablespoons mango chutney

1⅓ cups plain low-fat yogurt

1. In a medium saucepan, bring 2¼ cups of water to a boil. Add the rice and ¼ teaspoon of the salt, reduce to a simmer, cover, and cook until the rice is tender, about 17 minutes.

2. Meanwhile, in a medium saucepan of boiling water, cook the sweet potatoes until tender, about 10 minutes. Drain well.

3. In a large nonstick skillet or wok, heat the oil until hot but not smoking over medium heat. Add the cauliflower and stir-fry until lightly browned, about 3 minutes. Add the garlic and ginger and stir-fry until fragrant, about 1 minute. Add the tomatoes, curry powder, cumin, coriander, and chili powder, stirring well to combine. Add 1 cup of water and cook, stirring frequently, until the cauliflower is crisp-tender, about 4 minutes.

4. Stir in the sweet potatoes, chick-peas, spinach, chutney, and the remaining ½ teaspoon salt and cook, stirring frequently, until the potatoes are heated through and the spinach has wilted, about 3 minutes. Serve with the rice and yogurt.

Helpful hints: Mango chutney often contains large chunks of mango; for even flavoring, you may need to chop the chutney before using it in this dish. If you like, you can combine the sweet potatoes with 1½ cups of water in a microwave-safe bowl, cover, and microwave on high for about 10 minutes, or until the potatoes are cooked through.

FAT: 8G/15%
CALORIES: 487
SATURATED FAT: 1.5G
CARBOHYDRATE: 90G
PROTEIN: 17G
CHOLESTEROL: 5MG
SODIUM: 756MG

STIR-FRIED EGGPLANT WITH GARLIC AND CHEESE

SERVES: 4
WORKING TIME: 30 MINUTES
TOTAL TIME: 40 MINUTES

1 pound all-purpose potatoes, peeled and cut into ½-inch chunks

1 tablespoon olive oil

1 medium eggplant, cut into ½-inch chunks

2 leeks, halved lengthwise and cut into ½-inch slices, or 4 scallions, cut into ½-inch slices

5 cloves garlic, finely chopped

1 cup reduced-sodium chicken broth, defatted

¾ teaspoon salt

½ teaspoon dried rosemary

¼ teaspoon freshly ground black pepper

½ pound green beans, cut into 1-inch lengths

1 cup evaporated skimmed milk

2 teaspoons flour

½ cup shredded Swiss cheese (2 ounces)

1. In a medium pot of boiling water, cook the potatoes until firm-tender, about 10 minutes. Drain.

2. In a large nonstick skillet or wok, heat the oil until hot but not smoking over medium heat. Add the eggplant and stir-fry until lightly browned, about 3 minutes. Add the leeks, garlic, and ⅓ cup of the broth and cook, stirring frequently, until the leeks are softened, about 4 minutes. Add the potatoes, salt, rosemary, and pepper, and cook, stirring, until the leeks are tender, about 3 minutes.

3. Add the green beans to the pan and cook, stirring, until crisp-tender, about 4 minutes. In a medium bowl, whisk together the evaporated milk, the remaining ⅔ cup broth, and the flour. Add to the skillet and cook, stirring, until slightly thickened, about 2 minutes. Add the cheese and cook, stirring, until melted, about 1 minute. Divide among 4 plates and serve.

Helpful hint: A leek's many layers trap sand and dirt, and it's tricky to get a whole or split leek really clean. When the recipe calls for sliced leeks, like this one, it's easier to wash the vegetable in a bowl of water after cutting it up.

FAT: 8G/24%
CALORIES: 301
SATURATED FAT: 3.1G
CARBOHYDRATE: 46G
PROTEIN: 15G
CHOLESTEROL: 16MG
SODIUM: 709MG

VEGETABLES VINAIGRETTE WITH HERBED LENTILS

SERVES: 4
WORKING TIME: 45 MINUTES
TOTAL TIME: 45 MINUTES

Lentils provide the sturdy foundation for this one-dish meal. Unlike dried beans, lentils don't need to be presoaked, and they cook in less than half an hour; their subtle earthy flavor is the perfect foil for vegetables in a mustardy dressing. If you're in a rush to get dinner ready, pick up bags of ready-to-cook cauliflower and broccoli florets at the supermarket.

1 cup lentils, rinsed and picked over
1 red bell pepper, diced
¼ teaspoon salt
¼ teaspoon freshly ground black pepper
¼ teaspoon dried oregano
½ cup chopped fresh parsley
1 pound small red potatoes, halved (or quartered if large)
4 teaspoons olive oil
2 cups cauliflower florets
2 cups peeled baby carrots
2 cups broccoli florets
1½ cups reduced-sodium chicken broth, defatted
3 tablespoons fresh lemon juice
2 tablespoons Dijon mustard
1½ teaspoons cornstarch mixed with 1 tablespoon water

1. In a medium saucepan, bring 2¼ cups of water to a boil. Add the lentils, bell pepper, salt, black pepper, and oregano. Reduce to a simmer, cover, and cook until the lentils are just tender, about 25 minutes. Drain the lentils (if necessary) and stir in the parsley.

2. Meanwhile, in a separate saucepan of boiling water, cook the potatoes until almost tender, about 10 minutes. Drain. In a large non-stick skillet or wok, heat the oil until hot but not smoking over medium heat. Add the potatoes, cauliflower, and carrots and stir-fry until lightly browned, about 4 minutes. Add the broccoli and 1 cup of water and cook, stirring frequently, until the vegetables are tender, about 7 minutes.

3. In a small bowl, combine the broth, lemon juice, and mustard. Pour the broth mixture into the skillet and bring to a boil. Add the cornstarch mixture and cook, stirring, until slightly thickened, about 1 minute. Spoon the lentils onto 4 serving plates, top with the vegetable mixture, and serve.

Helpful hint: For extra flavor, cook the lentils in chicken broth rather than water.

FAT: 6G/14%
CALORIES: 378
SATURATED FAT: 0.7G
CARBOHYDRATE: 64G
PROTEIN: 21G
CHOLESTEROL: 0MG
SODIUM: 616MG

HOT SPINACH SALAD

SERVES: 4
WORKING TIME: 30 MINUTES
TOTAL TIME: 30 MINUTES

4 ounces crusty Italian or French bread, sliced ½ inch thick

2 cloves garlic, peeled and halved

1 tablespoon olive oil

3 tablespoons slivered Canadian bacon (1 ounce)

1 red onion, cut into ½-inch chunks

½ pound button mushrooms, thickly sliced

¼ pound fresh shiitake mushrooms, thickly sliced

2½ cups frozen corn kernels

1¼ pounds fresh spinach

1 cup reduced-sodium chicken broth, defatted

2 tablespoons balsamic or red wine vinegar

1 tablespoon Dijon mustard

2 teaspoons cornstarch mixed with 1 tablespoon water

1 tablespoon sesame seeds

1. Preheat the oven to 400°. Rub the bread slices with the garlic. Cut the bread into ½-inch cubes, place on a baking sheet, and bake until crisp, turning the croutons over once during baking, about 7 minutes.

2. Meanwhile, in a large nonstick skillet or wok, heat the oil until hot but not smoking over medium heat. Add the Canadian bacon and onion and stir-fry until the onion is crisp-tender, about 4 minutes. Add the button and shiitake mushrooms and stir-fry until the mushrooms begin to soften, about 4 minutes. Add the corn and stir-fry until heated through, about 2 minutes. Transfer the vegetables to a large salad bowl along with the croutons and spinach.

3. In a small bowl, whisk together the broth, vinegar, and mustard. Pour the mixture into the skillet and bring to a boil. Stir in the cornstarch mixture and cook, stirring, until slightly thickened, about 1 minute. Pour the hot dressing over the spinach and vegetables, tossing to combine. Sprinkle the sesame seeds on top and serve.

Helpful hint: Shiitake mushrooms are much more flavorful than button mushrooms, but if you can't find shiitakes, you can substitute another ¼ pound of button mushrooms.

FAT: 8G/24%
CALORIES: 307
SATURATED FAT: 1.2G
CARBOHYDRATE: 51G
PROTEIN: 15G
CHOLESTEROL: 4MG
SODIUM: 641MG

This update of spinach and bacon salad has much to recommend it. The main ingredient, nutrient-packed fresh spinach, keeps company with two kinds of sautéed mushrooms, golden corn kernels, and garlicky croutons. For a healthier salad, leaner Canadian bacon takes the place of regular sliced bacon, and the aromatic warm vinaigrette is fat-free.

MOO SHU VEGETABLES

SERVES: 4
WORKING TIME: 40 MINUTES
TOTAL TIME: 40 MINUTES

Although most commonly associated with a pork dish, the term "moo shu" can be applied with equal accuracy to this splendid vegetarian spread. Instead of the traditional Mandarin pancakes (made by rolling out a dough into paper-thin circles), we use crêpes, which are much simpler to prepare.

1½ cups low-fat (1%) milk
1 cup flour
½ teaspoon sugar
½ teaspoon salt
1 tablespoon vegetable oil
3 scallions, thinly sliced
1 tablespoon finely chopped fresh ginger
1 red bell pepper, cut into thin strips
2 cups julienne-cut butternut squash
6 ounces button mushrooms, thinly sliced
¼ pound fresh shiitake mushrooms, thinly sliced
½ pound firm tofu, cut into ½-inch cubes
3 tablespoons reduced-sodium soy sauce
2 tablespoons rice vinegar
2 tablespoons plum jam
½ teaspoon cornstarch mixed with 2 teaspoons water

1. In a small bowl, whisk the milk into the flour until well combined. Add the sugar and ¼ teaspoon of the salt and whisk again until smooth. Spray a small (6-inch) nonstick skillet with nonstick cooking spray and set over medium heat.

2. Pour a scant ¼ cup of the batter into the pan, tilting it so that the crêpe spreads to cover the bottom of the pan. Cook until lightly browned on one side and cooked through, about 30 seconds. Transfer to a plate, cover with waxed paper, and repeat with the remaining batter, separating the crêpes with waxed paper, for a total of 8 crêpes.

3. In a large nonstick skillet or wok, heat the oil until hot but not smoking over medium heat. Add the scallions and ginger and stir-fry until fragrant, about 1 minute. Add the bell pepper and stir-fry until crisp-tender, about 3 minutes. Add the butternut squash, button mushrooms, and shiitake mushrooms and stir-fry until tender, about 5 minutes. Add the tofu and toss gently to combine.

4. In a small bowl, combine the soy sauce, vinegar, jam, the remaining ¼ teaspoon salt, and ¼ cup of water. Stir into the vegetable mixture and bring to a boil. Add the cornstarch mixture and cook, stirring, until slightly thickened, about 1 minute. Divide the crêpes among 4 plates and spoon the vegetable mixture over the crêpes. Roll up or leave open-face and serve.

FAT: 10G/25%
CALORIES: 359
SATURATED FAT: 1.8G
CARBOHYDRATE: 53G
PROTEIN: 19G
CHOLESTEROL: 4MG
SODIUM: 790MG

S ummer suppers in Provence often include ratatouille, a colorful meatless "stew" of fresh tomatoes, eggplant, peppers, and squash. Topped with goat cheese and accompanied with pasta, this ratatouille is a meal in itself. You don't have to serve the ratatouille straight from the stove; it's quite delicious at room temperature and makes tempting picnic fare.

RATATOUILLE STIR-FRY WITH GOAT CHEESE

SERVES: 4
WORKING TIME: 30 MINUTES
TOTAL TIME: 30 MINUTES

6 ounces orzo pasta

1 tablespoon olive oil

1 red onion, coarsely diced

4 cloves garlic, finely chopped

1 red bell pepper, cut into thin strips

1 zucchini, cut into 2-by-½-inch strips

1 yellow summer squash, cut into 2-by-½-inch strips

1 small eggplant, cut into 2-by-½-inch strips (see tip)

5½-ounce can low-sodium tomato-vegetable juice

1½ cups cherry tomatoes, halved

2 teaspoons capers, rinsed and drained

¾ teaspoon dried tarragon

¾ teaspoon salt

¼ cup chopped fresh basil

3 ounces goat cheese or feta cheese, crumbled

1. In a large pot of boiling water, cook the pasta until just tender. Drain well.

2. Meanwhile, in a large nonstick skillet or wok, heat the oil until hot but not smoking over medium heat. Add the onion and garlic and stir-fry until the onion is slightly softened, about 2 minutes. Add the bell pepper, zucchini, and yellow squash and stir-fry until crisp-tender, about 4 minutes.

3. Add the eggplant and stir-fry until lightly browned, about 4 minutes. Add the tomato-vegetable juice, tomatoes, capers, tarragon, and salt and cook until the tomatoes are softened, about 4 minutes. Stir in the basil. Divide the orzo among 4 plates. Spoon the vegetables over the orzo, sprinkle the cheese on top, and serve.

Helpful hint: If you can't get low-sodium tomato-vegetable juice, use regular tomato-vegetable juice and reduce the salt in the recipe to ½ teaspoon.

TIP

To cut an eggplant into strips, first cut it crosswise into ½-inch-thick slices. Stack several slices, and then cut through the stack to create ½-inch-wide strips.

FAT: 11G/29%
CALORIES: 347
SATURATED FAT: 5G
CARBOHYDRATE: 51G
PROTEIN: 14G
CHOLESTEROL: 17MG
SODIUM: 606MG

Vegetable Fajitas

Serves: 4
Working time: 30 minutes
Total time: 30 minutes

These meatless fajitas—based on a mixture of vegetables, black beans, and spices rather than beef or chicken—are quite a departure from the original recipe, but are no less delicious. As always, fajitas can make an appealing "hands on" meal: Bring the skillet, warmed tortillas, and cheese to the table for do-it-yourself assembly. Offer extra salsa on the side.

2 teaspoons olive oil

4 scallions, thinly sliced

3 cloves garlic, finely chopped

2 zucchini, halved lengthwise and thinly sliced

2 yellow summer squash, halved lengthwise and thinly sliced

16-ounce can black beans, rinsed and drained

½ cup mild or medium-hot prepared salsa

1 tomato, coarsely chopped

1½ cups frozen corn kernels

2 tablespoons fresh lime juice

½ teaspoon dried oregano

½ teaspoon hot pepper sauce

Eight 8-inch flour tortillas

½ cup shredded Monterey jack cheese (2 ounces)

1. In a large nonstick skillet or wok, heat the oil until hot but not smoking over medium heat. Add the scallions and garlic and stir-fry until fragrant, about 1 minute. Add the zucchini and yellow squash and stir-fry until crisp-tender, about 4 minutes.

2. Add the beans, salsa, tomato, corn, lime juice, oregano, and hot pepper sauce and cook, stirring frequently, until just heated through, about 3 minutes.

3. Meanwhile, preheat the oven to 400°. Wrap the tortillas in foil and heat just until warm, about 5 minutes. Place 2 tortillas on each of 4 plates. Spoon the vegetables onto the tortillas, sprinkle with the cheese, and roll up the tortillas or serve open-face.

Helpful hint: Monterey jack is a semisoft, cream-colored cheese with a mildly tangy flavor. Dry jack, the aged version of the same cheese, is a grating cheese rather like a cross between Cheddar and Parmesan.

Fat: 13g/24%
Calories: 479
Saturated Fat: 3.8g
Carbohydrate: 74g
Protein: 18g
Cholesterol: 15mg
Sodium: 941mg

SAUTÉED MARINATED TOFU

SERVES: 4
WORKING TIME: 40 MINUTES
TOTAL TIME: 40 MINUTES PLUS MARINATING TIME

Infused with soy and citrus, the triangles of tofu develop a crisp crust when sautéed. Marinate them overnight, if possible.

¾ teaspoon grated orange zest

⅓ cup orange juice

¼ cup reduced-sodium soy sauce

1 tablespoon minced fresh ginger

2 cloves garlic, finely chopped

1 tablespoon firmly packed light brown sugar

1 teaspoon cornstarch

1 large cake of firm tofu (¾ pound), cut into 4 triangles (see helpful hint)

1¼ pounds sweet potatoes, peeled and cut into ½-inch chunks

1 tablespoon vegetable oil

1 red bell pepper, cut into 1-inch squares

1 green bell pepper, cut into 1-inch squares

8-ounce can sliced water chestnuts, drained

2 cups bean sprouts

¼ teaspoon salt

2 scallions, thinly sliced

1. In a medium bowl, combine the orange zest, orange juice, soy sauce, ginger, garlic, brown sugar, and cornstarch. Add the tofu, spooning the marinade over. Cover and let stand for at least 30 minutes at room temperature or for up to 12 hours in the refrigerator.

2. In a medium pot of boiling water, cook the sweet potatoes until firm-tender, about 7 minutes. Drain well. In a large nonstick skillet, heat the oil until hot but not smoking over medium heat. Reserving the marinade, add the tofu to the pan and cook until the tofu is light brown and crisp, about 3 minutes per side. With a slotted spoon or spatula, transfer the tofu to a plate.

3. Add the bell peppers to the skillet and cook, stirring, until crisp-tender, about 3 minutes. Add the sweet potatoes, water chestnuts, bean sprouts, and salt and cook, stirring, until the vegetables are heated through, about 4 minutes. Add the reserved marinade and cook, stirring, until slightly thickened, about 1 minute. Spoon the vegetables onto 4 plates and top with the tofu. Sprinkle the scallions over the tofu and serve.

Helpful hint: To form the triangular serving pieces of tofu, first cut the cake of tofu crosswise on the diagonal to make two thick triangles; then, cut the triangles horizontally into thinner slices.

FAT: 11G/29%
CALORIES: 344
SATURATED FAT: 1.6G
CARBOHYDRATE: 47G
PROTEIN: 19G
CHOLESTEROL: 0MG
SODIUM: 771MG

WINTER VEGETABLE STIR-FRY WITH BEANS

SERVES: 4
WORKING TIME: 35 MINUTES
TOTAL TIME: 35 MINUTES

1 pound all-purpose potatoes, peeled and cut into ½-inch chunks

1 tablespoon olive oil

2 leeks, halved lengthwise and cut into ½-inch slices, or 4 scallions, cut into ½-inch slices

3 cloves garlic, finely chopped

2 carrots, halved lengthwise and cut into ½-inch pieces

1 celery root (10 ounces), peeled and cut into ½-inch chunks

2 ribs celery, cut into ½-inch slices

½ teaspoon salt

½ teaspoon dried rosemary

½ teaspoon dried tarragon

¼ teaspoon freshly ground black pepper

15-ounce can pinto beans, rinsed and drained

⅓ cup reduced-fat sour cream

¼ cup plain nonfat yogurt

2 teaspoons flour

1. In a medium pot of boiling water, cook the potatoes until firm-tender, about 7 minutes. Drain, reserving 1⅓ cups of the cooking liquid.

2. In a large nonstick skillet or wok, heat the oil until hot but not smoking over medium heat. Add the leeks and garlic and stir-fry until the leeks are crisp-tender, about 2 minutes. Add the carrots and celery root and stir-fry until the celery root is lightly browned, about 5 minutes. Add ⅓ cup of the reserved potato cooking liquid and cook, stirring frequently, until the celery root is crisp-tender, about 4 minutes.

3. Add the celery, salt, rosemary, tarragon, and pepper and cook, stirring, until fragrant, about 1 minute. Add the beans, potatoes, and the remaining 1 cup potato cooking liquid and cook, stirring frequently, until the vegetables are tender, about 5 minutes.

4. Meanwhile, in a small bowl, combine the sour cream, yogurt, and flour. Add the sour cream mixture to the pan, and cook, stirring, just until the vegetables are well coated, about 1 minute.

Helpful hint: Celery ribs and celery root come from two distinct varieties of celery. Celery root, also called celeriac, is grown for its knobby, baseball-sized root. It has a strong celery flavor and a texture something like a turnip.

FAT: 7G/22%
CALORIES: 283
SATURATED FAT: 1.9G
CARBOHYDRATE: 47G
PROTEIN: 10G
CHOLESTEROL: 7MG
SODIUM: 574MG

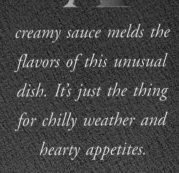

A creamy sauce melds the flavors of this unusual dish. It's just the thing for chilly weather and hearty appetites.

PAN-FRIED RAVIOLI WITH VEGETABLES

SERVES: 4
WORKING TIME: 20 MINUTES
TOTAL TIME: 20 MINUTES

Sautéing ravioli gives this familiar filled pasta an appetizing new texture and taste. The pan-fried ravioli, delicately browned and slightly crisped, are tossed with an Italian-style vegetable medley that includes green beans, tomatoes, and cannellini. Other small filled pastas, such as tortellini or cappelletti, can be cooked in the same way.

¾ pound fresh small cheese ravioli

1 tablespoon olive oil

2 scallions, thinly sliced

4 cloves garlic, finely chopped

10-ounce package frozen Italian flat green beans, thawed

2 tomatoes, coarsely chopped

19-ounce can white kidney beans (cannellini), rinsed and drained

½ cup raisins

1 tablespoon no-salt-added tomato paste

¼ cup chopped fresh basil

¼ teaspoon salt

¼ teaspoon freshly ground black pepper

⅛ teaspoon cayenne pepper

1. In a large pot of boiling water, cook the ravioli until just tender. Drain, reserving 1 cup of the cooking liquid. Pat the ravioli dry on paper towels.

2. In a large nonstick skillet or wok, heat the oil until hot but not smoking over medium heat. Add the ravioli to the pan and gently stir-fry until lightly crisped and golden on both sides, about 4 minutes. With a slotted spoon, transfer the ravioli to a plate.

3. Add the scallions and garlic to the skillet and stir-fry until softened, about 1 minute. Add the green beans, stirring to coat. Add the tomatoes, white kidney beans, raisins, tomato paste, basil, salt, black pepper, cayenne, and the reserved ravioli cooking liquid and bring to a boil. Cook, stirring frequently, until slightly thickened, about 3 minutes. Return the ravioli to the pan, tossing to coat well, and cook until heated through, about 1 minute.

Helpful hint: When local tomatoes are not in season, the best choice at the market may well be plum tomatoes. If you do opt for this smaller variety, use three instead of two.

FAT: 16G/29%
CALORIES: 501
SATURATED FAT: 6.5G
CARBOHYDRATE: 71G
PROTEIN: 23G
CHOLESTEROL: 75MG
SODIUM: 677MG

The
Alsace region of France
borders Germany, so it
should come as no
surprise that Alsatian
food is renowned for
its heartiness as well
as its lush flavors.
Here, the combination
of noodles, cabbage,
and apple reflects this
German influence.
Even without long
cooking, these
ingredients readily take
on the smoky goodness
of Canadian bacon.

ALSATIAN CABBAGE AND NOODLE STIR-FRY

SERVES: 4
WORKING TIME: 25 MINUTES
TOTAL TIME: 35 MINUTES

8 ounces wide egg noodles

1 tablespoon olive oil

3 tablespoons slivered Canadian bacon (1 ounce)

1 large onion, coarsely chopped

¾ pound Savoy cabbage, cut into 1-inch chunks (see tip)

1 large McIntosh, Cortland, or Empire apple, cored and cut into ½-inch chunks

¾ teaspoon salt

½ teaspoon freshly ground black pepper

⅓ cup reduced-fat sour cream

3 tablespoons plain nonfat yogurt

2 teaspoons flour

½ cup snipped fresh dill

1. In a large pot of boiling water, cook the noodles until just tender. Drain well.

2. In a large nonstick skillet or wok, heat the oil until hot but not smoking over medium heat. Add the Canadian bacon and onion and stir-fry until the bacon is lightly browned and the onion is crisp-tender, about 4 minutes. Add the cabbage, apple, salt, and pepper and stir-fry until the apple is crisp-tender, about 4 minutes. Stir in the noodles and stir-fry until lightly browned, about 4 minutes.

3. In a small bowl, combine the sour cream, yogurt, and flour. Add the sour cream mixture to the skillet and cook, stirring, until slightly thickened, about 1 minute. Stir in the dill, divide among 4 plates, and serve.

Helpful hint: Savoy cabbage is a green cabbage with very crinkly leaves. Its unique texture makes this dish special, but regular green cabbage could be used instead.

FAT: 9G/22%
CALORIES: 375
SATURATED FAT: 2.5G
CARBOHYDRATE: 61G
PROTEIN: 14G
CHOLESTEROL: 64MG
SODIUM: 571MG

TIP

To prepare the cabbage for this recipe, first halve the head and cut out the dense white core. Cut the cabbage half into 1-inch-wide wedges, then cut the wedges crosswise into 1-inch pieces.

VEGETABLE CHOW MEIN

SERVES: 4
WORKING TIME: 30 MINUTES
TOTAL TIME: 30 MINUTES

Although "chow mein" is an authentic Cantonese dish, it has been in this country for so long (probably since the early 1850s) that it has nearly achieved traditional American cuisine status. Basically a noodle stir-fry, it can include all manner of ingredients; here we present a light, meatless version made with fettuccine in place of the usual fresh Chinese egg noodles.

8 ounces fettuccine

1 tablespoon dark Oriental sesame oil

6 scallions, thinly sliced

4 cloves garlic, finely chopped

2 tablespoons finely chopped fresh ginger

1 red bell pepper, cut into thin strips

1 green bell pepper, cut into thin strips

2 ribs celery, cut into ¼-inch slices

½ pound button mushrooms, halved

¼ teaspoon salt

2 teaspoons cornstarch

¾ cup reduced-sodium chicken broth, defatted

3 tablespoons reduced-sodium soy sauce

2 tablespoons dry sherry

1 tablespoon fresh lemon juice

1. In a large pot of boiling water, cook the fettuccine until just tender. Drain well.

2. Meanwhile, in a large nonstick skillet or wok, heat 2 teaspoons of the sesame oil until hot but not smoking over medium heat. Add the scallions, garlic, and ginger and stir-fry until the scallions are crisp-tender, about 1 minute. Add the bell peppers, celery, and mushrooms and stir-fry until the bell peppers and celery are crisp-tender, about 4 minutes. Add the pasta to the skillet and stir-fry until lightly crisped, about 1 minute.

3. In a small bowl, combine the salt, cornstarch, broth, soy sauce, sherry, lemon juice, and the remaining 1 teaspoon oil. Pour the mixture into the skillet and cook, stirring, until slightly thickened, about 1 minute.

Helpful hint: You can cut up the bell peppers and celery a few hours ahead of time; combine them in a sealable bag or a covered bowl and refrigerate until needed.

FAT: 6G/17%
CALORIES: 313
SATURATED FAT: 1G
CARBOHYDRATE: 52G
PROTEIN: 12G
CHOLESTEROL: 54MG
SODIUM: 744MG

VEGETARIAN CHEESEBURGERS

SERVES: 4
WORKING TIME: 20 MINUTES
TOTAL TIME: 30 MINUTES PLUS SOAKING TIME

Veggie burgers made from nuts are high in fat. Our bean-based burger has a meaty flavor and impressively healthy "numbers."

2 cups boiling water
½ cup bulghur (cracked wheat)
Two 16-ounce cans pinto beans, rinsed and drained
2 tablespoons fresh lime juice
1½ teaspoons ground coriander
½ teaspoon cayenne pepper
1 red bell pepper, finely chopped
1 yellow bell pepper, finely chopped
4 scallions, thinly sliced
¼ cup ketchup
4 teaspoons olive oil
¼ cup flour
¾ cup shredded Monterey jack cheese (3 ounces)
4 hamburger buns
8 leaves of Boston lettuce

1. In a medium bowl, combine the boiling water and bulghur and set aside to soften for 30 minutes. Drain. In a large bowl, combine the beans with the drained bulghur. With a potato masher, mash the beans and bulghur until almost smooth with some lumps remaining. Add the lime juice, coriander, and cayenne, stirring to combine. Add ½ cup of the red bell pepper, ½ cup of the yellow bell pepper, and ¼ cup of the scallions. Shape into 4 patties 4 inches in diameter.

2. In a small bowl, combine the ketchup, and the remaining bell peppers and scallions. Set aside.

3. In a large nonstick skillet, heat the oil until hot but not smoking over medium heat. Dredge the patties in the flour, shaking off the excess. Sauté the patties until crisp on the outside and heated through, about 4 minutes per side. Sprinkle the cheese on top, cover, and cook until the cheese is melted, about 1 minute. Divide the buns among 4 plates. Place 2 lettuce leaves on each of the buns, top with a patty and the ketchup mixture, and serve.

Helpful hints: If you're not used to cayenne, start with just ¼ teaspoon (or even less) and gradually add more if necessary. Brighten the plate with a garnish of red radishes or cherry tomatoes.

FAT: 15G/27%
CALORIES: 495
SATURATED FAT: 5G
CARBOHYDRATE: 71G
PROTEIN: 21G
CHOLESTEROL: 23MG
SODIUM: 908MG

FISH & SHELLFISH

4

If
you're looking for a
quick meal with flair,
search no further.
Sweet, delicate scallops
are always a treat;
dusted with cumin,
sautéed with vegetables,
and served over freshly
cooked linguine, they
make a fine dinner for
family or friends.
Partner the main dish
with a salad of dark
leafy greens and cherry
tomatoes.

SPICY SCALLOPS WITH LINGUINE

SERVES: 4
WORKING TIME: 30 MINUTES
TOTAL TIME: 30 MINUTES

8 ounces linguine

1 tablespoon flour

1 teaspoon ground cumin

¼ teaspoon salt

¼ teaspoon freshly ground black
pepper

1 pound bay scallops or
quartered sea scallops (see tip)

1 tablespoon olive oil

1 cup sliced scallions

1 clove garlic, minced

1 zucchini, cut into ¼-inch dice

1 yellow summer squash, cut into
¼-inch dice

2 tomatoes, diced

1 small fresh or pickled jalapeño
pepper, seeded and minced

½ cup reduced-sodium chicken
broth, defatted

1. In a large pot of boiling water, cook the linguine until just tender. Drain well.

2. Meanwhile, in a sturdy plastic bag, combine the flour, cumin, salt, and pepper. Add the scallops to the bag, tossing to coat. In a large nonstick skillet or wok, heat 2 teaspoons of the oil until hot but not smoking over medium-high heat. Add the scallops and stir-fry until the scallops are just opaque, 2 to 3 minutes. With a slotted spoon, transfer the scallops to a plate.

3. Add the remaining 1 teaspoon oil to the skillet. Add the scallions and garlic and stir-fry until the scallions are softened, about 1 minute. Add the zucchini, summer squash, tomatoes, jalapeño, and broth and bring to a boil. Cook, stirring, until the squash is crisp-tender, about 3 minutes. Return the scallops to the pan and cook until heated through, about 1 minute.

4. Divide the pasta among 4 plates, spoon the scallops and sauce over, and serve.

Helpful hints: It's best to buy scallops no longer than one day before you plan to use them. Before dredging them in the flour mixture, use paper towels to pat the scallops dry.

TIP

If the smaller and sweeter bay scallops are not available, use the larger sea scallops. Cut each one into quarters so they are about the same size as the bay variety.

FAT: 6G/14%
CALORIES: 389
SATURATED FAT: 0.7G
CARBOHYDRATE: 55G
PROTEIN: 29G
CHOLESTEROL: 38MG
SODIUM: 415MG

SAUTÉED RED SNAPPER WITH ONION RELISH

SERVES: 4
WORKING TIME: 20 MINUTES
TOTAL TIME: 20 MINUTES

1 red onion, diced

1 red or yellow bell pepper, diced

6 pimiento-stuffed green olives (1 ounce), chopped

2 tablespoons chopped fresh mint

¼ cup fresh lime juice

4 teaspoons honey

1 tablespoon balsamic vinegar

½ teaspoon salt

4 skinless red snapper fillets (about 6 ounces each), any visible bones removed

1 teaspoon paprika

2 tablespoons flour

1 tablespoon olive oil

1. In a small bowl, combine the onion and ice water to cover. In a medium bowl, combine the bell pepper, olives, mint, 3 tablespoons of the lime juice, the honey, vinegar, and ¼ teaspoon of the salt. Set both bowls aside while you prepare the fish.

2. Sprinkle both sides of the snapper with the remaining 1 tablespoon lime juice, the paprika, and the remaining ¼ teaspoon salt. Place the flour on a sheet of waxed paper. Dredge the fillets in the flour, shaking off the excess.

3. In a large nonstick skillet, heat the oil until hot but not smoking over medium heat. Add the snapper and cook until lightly browned and just cooked through, about 2 minutes per side.

4. Meanwhile, drain the onion, pat dry, and add to the bowl with the bell pepper mixture; stir to combine. Serve the snapper with the relish.

Helpful hints: Brief soaking in ice water tames the onion's bite—a point to remember whenever you're using raw onions for salads or sandwiches. You can substitute any firm-fleshed white fish, such as striped bass or sole, for the red snapper, if you like.

FAT: 7G/23%
CALORIES: 273
SATURATED FAT: 1G
CARBOHYDRATE: 16G
PROTEIN: 36G
CHOLESTEROL: 63MG
SODIUM: 558MG

When you're sautéing fish fillets, it helps to dredge them in flour—otherwise it's all too easy for the fish to stick to the pan. A dusting of flour also produces just a suggestion of a crisp crust, which offers a pleasing contrast to the tender fish. These meaty snapper fillets are topped with a sweet-and-tangy relish of diced bell pepper, onion, and green olives.

FLOUNDER WITH TOMATO "MAYONNAISE"

SERVES: 4
WORKING TIME: 25 MINUTES
TOTAL TIME: 25 MINUTES

The thick, garlicky "mayonnaise" for this flounder sauté makes a wonderful low-fat alternative to tartar sauce. Studded with bits of fresh tomato and scallion, our sauce is based on a purée of white kidney beans with nonfat yogurt and a little reduced-fat mayo added for creaminess. Round out the meal with a side of roasted potatoes.

1 clove garlic

1 cup canned white kidney beans (cannellini), rinsed and drained

¼ cup plain nonfat yogurt

2 tablespoons reduced-fat mayonnaise

2 tablespoons fresh lemon juice

¾ teaspoon salt

⅛ teaspoon hot pepper sauce

4 plum tomatoes, coarsely diced

1 tablespoon flour

¼ teaspoon freshly ground black pepper

4 flounder fillets (about 4 ounces each), any visible bones removed

1 tablespoon vegetable oil

½ cup sliced scallions

1. In a small saucepan of boiling water, cook the garlic for 1 minute to blanch. Rinse under cold water and remove the skin. Place the garlic in a food processor or blender along with the beans, yogurt, mayonnaise, 1 tablespoon of the lemon juice, ½ teaspoon of the salt, and the hot pepper sauce. Process to a smooth purée. Transfer the mixture to a bowl and stir in half of the diced tomatoes. Set aside.

2. On a sheet of waxed paper, combine the flour, pepper, and the remaining ¼ teaspoon salt. Dredge the fillets in the flour mixture, shaking off the excess. In a large nonstick skillet, heat the oil until hot but not smoking over medium-high heat. Add the fish and cook until just opaque, about 2 minutes per side.

3. Meanwhile, in a small bowl, combine the remaining tomatoes with the scallions. Divide the fish among 4 plates and sprinkle with the remaining 1 tablespoon lemon juice. Top with the tomato "mayonnaise" and tomato-scallion mixture and serve.

Helpful hints: You can make the mayonnaise in advance up to the point of adding the tomatoes: Refrigerate the sauce for up to 12 hours. At serving time, stir in the tomatoes. You can substitute any firm-fleshed white fish, such as striped bass or red snapper, for the flounder, if you like.

FAT: 7G/27%
CALORIES: 233
SATURATED FAT: 1G
CARBOHYDRATE: 16G
PROTEIN: 27G
CHOLESTEROL: 55MG
SODIUM: 671MG

*T*he flavor and fragrance of oregano are abundant but not overpowering in this adaptation of an Italian standard; lemon and fresh parsley in the sauce temper the intensity of the dried herb. Oregano can turn bitter if it scorches or burns, so be sure to keep stirring after adding the shrimp, zucchini, and seasonings to the pan.

SHRIMP OREGANATA

SERVES: 4
WORKING TIME: 35 MINUTES
TOTAL TIME: 35 MINUTES

¼ cup chopped fresh parsley

1 teaspoon grated lemon zest

½ teaspoon salt

4 teaspoons olive oil

6 ounces orzo pasta

3 cloves garlic, finely chopped

1 pound medium shrimp, shelled and deveined (see tip)

1 zucchini, halved lengthwise and cut into ¼-inch slices

¾ teaspoon dried oregano

1½ cups cherry tomatoes, halved

⅔ cup bottled clam juice, or reduced-sodium chicken broth, defatted

3 tablespoons fresh lemon juice

2 teaspoons cornstarch mixed with 1 tablespoon water

1. In a medium bowl, combine 2 tablespoons of the parsley, ½ teaspoon of the lemon zest, ¼ teaspoon of the salt, and 1 teaspoon of the oil; set aside.

2. In a medium pot of boiling water, cook the pasta until just tender. Drain well. Add the pasta to the bowl with the parsley mixture and toss to combine. Cover and set aside.

3. Meanwhile, in a large nonstick skillet or wok, heat the remaining 1 tablespoon oil until hot but not smoking over medium heat. Add the garlic and stir-fry until softened, about 1 minute. Add the shrimp, zucchini, oregano, the remaining ½ teaspoon lemon zest, and remaining ¼ teaspoon salt and stir-fry until the shrimp are almost opaque throughout, about 3 minutes.

4. Add the tomatoes, clam juice, and lemon juice and bring to a boil. Add the cornstarch mixture and cook, stirring, until the sauce is slightly thickened, about 1 minute. Stir in the remaining 2 tablespoons parsley and serve with the orzo.

Helpful hint: The simple, light pasta "dressing" made in step 1 can be used anytime you're serving pasta as a side dish. For variety's sake, you could mix the oil, lemon zest, and salt with fresh herbs other than parsley—such as basil, mint, or cilantro.

FAT: 7G/20%
CALORIES: 323
SATURATED FAT: 1G
CARBOHYDRATE: 39G
PROTEIN: 25G
CHOLESTEROL: 140MG
SODIUM: 506MG

TIP

To shell fresh shrimp, pull apart the shell at the belly of the shrimp with your fingers, splitting the shell, and remove. Leave the tail portion attached, if desired, for a garnish. To devein, using the point of a sharp knife, score the shrimp along the back, then remove the dark vein.

SAUTÉED SWORDFISH WITH FRESH TOMATO SAUCE

SERVES: 4
WORKING TIME: 30 MINUTES
TOTAL TIME: 35 MINUTES

Not every type of fish would be suited to a robust tomato sauce, but swordfish, with its firm, beefy texture, is the perfect partner for this fresh-tomato topping. The chunky sauce is dotted with capers and flavored with garlic and orange zest. We serve the fish with orzo, but you can use another pasta shape if you like. Or serve the swordfish with grains, such as a mix of white and wild rice.

8 ounces orzo pasta

1 tablespoon flour

1 teaspoon fennel seeds, crushed, or ½ teaspoon ground fennel

½ teaspoon ground coriander

¾ teaspoon salt

⅛ teaspoon cayenne pepper

4 small swordfish steaks (about 4 ounces each)

1 tablespoon vegetable oil

2 shallots, finely chopped, or ⅓ cup chopped scallion whites

2 cloves garlic, minced

2 tomatoes, coarsely diced

¼ cup reduced-sodium chicken broth, defatted

2 tablespoons capers, rinsed, drained, and chopped

½ teaspoon grated orange zest

¼ teaspoon sugar

1. In a medium pot of boiling water, cook the pasta until just tender. Drain well.

2. Meanwhile, on a sheet of waxed paper, combine the flour, fennel, coriander, ¼ teaspoon of the salt, and the cayenne. Dredge the swordfish in the flour mixture, shaking off the excess. In a large nonstick skillet, heat 2 teaspoons of the oil until hot but not smoking over medium-high heat. Add the swordfish and cook until just opaque throughout, about 3 minutes per side. Transfer the swordfish to a plate and cover loosely with foil to keep warm.

3. Add the remaining 1 teaspoon oil to the skillet. Add the shallots and garlic and cook, stirring, until the shallots begin to brown, about 1 minute. Stir in the tomatoes, broth, capers, orange zest, sugar, and the remaining ½ teaspoon salt. Cook until the liquid is slightly reduced and the tomatoes have softened, about 3 minutes.

4. Divide the orzo among 4 plates. Place the swordfish alongside, top with the sauce, and serve.

Helpful hints: Use a mortar and pestle to crush whole fennel seeds. Tuna steaks can be substituted for the swordfish, if you like.

FAT: 9G/21%
CALORIES: 392
SATURATED FAT: 1.7G
CARBOHYDRATE: 49G
PROTEIN: 28G
CHOLESTEROL: 39MG
SODIUM: 664MG

STIR-FRIED SWORDFISH TERIYAKI

SERVES: 4
WORKING TIME: 25 MINUTES
TOTAL TIME: 25 MINUTES

Teriyaki marinade, a lightly sweetened mixture of wine and soy sauce, flavors the fish and vegetables in this delectable stir-fry.

1 cup long-grain rice

¼ teaspoon salt

¼ cup dry white wine or dry sherry

3 tablespoons reduced-sodium soy sauce

2 tablespoons fresh lemon juice

1 tablespoon firmly packed light brown sugar

1 teaspoon cornstarch

1 tablespoon dark Oriental sesame oil

4 scallions, cut into 1-inch lengths

2 cloves garlic, finely chopped

1 tablespoon finely chopped fresh ginger

2 cups mushrooms, halved

1 large carrot, cut into 2-by-⅛-inch julienne strips

1 pound swordfish steaks, skinned and cut into 1-inch chunks

¼ pound snow peas, cut lengthwise into thin strips

1. In a medium saucepan, bring 2¼ cups of water to a boil. Add the rice and salt, reduce to a simmer, cover, and cook until the rice is tender, about 17 minutes.

2. Meanwhile, in a small bowl, combine the wine, soy sauce, lemon juice, brown sugar, and cornstarch. In a large nonstick skillet or wok, heat the oil until hot but not smoking over medium heat. Add the scallions, garlic, and ginger and stir-fry until the scallions are softened, about 2 minutes. Add the mushrooms and carrot and stir-fry until the carrot is crisp-tender, about 4 minutes.

3. Add the swordfish to the skillet and stir-fry until almost opaque throughout, about 3 minutes. Stir the soy mixture to recombine and add to the skillet along with the snow peas. Cook, stirring, until the swordfish is cooked through and the snow peas are crisp-tender, about 1 minute. Divide the rice among 4 plates, spoon the swordfish over, and serve.

Helpful hint: You can make the teriyaki sauce up to 12 hours in advance; store it in a covered jar in the refrigerator and shake it before adding it to the skillet.

FAT: 8G/18%
CALORIES: 395
SATURATED FAT: 1.7G
CARBOHYDRATE: 51G
PROTEIN: 26G
CHOLESTEROL: 39MG
SODIUM: 695MG

RED SNAPPER WITH CHILI-CORN SALSA

SERVES: 4
WORKING TIME: 20 MINUTES
TOTAL TIME: 25 MINUTES

2 teaspoons chili powder

1 teaspoon ground cumin

1 teaspoon ground coriander

½ teaspoon salt

1½ cups frozen corn kernels, thawed

1 tomato, diced

3 scallions, thinly sliced

1 pickled jalapeño pepper, seeded and finely chopped

2 tablespoons balsamic or red wine vinegar

4 skinless red snapper fillets (about 6 ounces each), any visible bones removed

2 tablespoons flour

1 tablespoon olive oil

1. In a medium bowl, combine the chili powder, cumin, coriander, and salt. Remove 2 teaspoons of the mixture and set aside. Stir the corn, tomato, scallions, jalapeño, and vinegar into the mixture remaining in the bowl.

2. Rub the reserved spice mixture onto both sides of the red snapper fillets. Place the flour on a sheet of waxed paper. Dredge the snapper in the flour, shaking off the excess. In a large nonstick skillet, heat the oil until hot but not smoking over medium heat. Add the snapper and cook until lightly browned and just opaque, about 3 minutes per side. Divide the snapper among 4 plates, spoon the salsa over, and serve.

Helpful hints: You can substitute any firm-fleshed white fish, such as flounder or sole, for the red snapper. If you like the blend of chili powder, cumin, and coriander, try mixing up some extra to rub on chicken breasts, turkey cutlets, and other meats and poultry before sautéing, broiling, or grilling.

FAT: 7G/22%
CALORIES: 286
SATURATED FAT: 1G
CARBOHYDRATE: 19G
PROTEIN: 38G
CHOLESTEROL: 63MG
SODIUM: 458MG

Toss a salad to serve with this zesty Mexican-style dish. The snapper is rubbed with chili, cumin, and coriander.

SHRIMP SAUTÉ PRIMAVERA

SERVES: 4
WORKING TIME: 35 MINUTES
TOTAL TIME: 35 MINUTES

*G*reen, yellow, orange, and red vegetables enliven this innovative pasta dish. Pasta primavera has, of course, been around for years, but the vegetables are traditionally blanched, not stir-fried—and you won't find the bright flavors of lemon and fresh ginger in the original recipe either. The addition of shrimp makes this pasta dish a delicious, substantial meal.

6 ounces angel hair pasta

4 cloves garlic, finely chopped

1 tablespoon finely chopped fresh ginger

½ teaspoon dried rosemary

1 teaspoon grated lemon zest

¾ teaspoon salt

1 pound medium shrimp, shelled and deveined

1 tablespoon olive oil

1 large carrot, thinly sliced

1 red bell pepper, cut into ½-inch squares

1 yellow summer squash, halved lengthwise and thinly sliced

2 cups small broccoli florets

1 cup bottled clam juice, or reduced-sodium chicken broth, defatted

2 tablespoons fresh lemon juice

1½ teaspoons cornstarch mixed with 1 tablespoon water

1. In a large pot of boiling water, cook the pasta until just tender. Drain well.

2. Meanwhile, in a large bowl, combine the garlic, ginger, rosemary, lemon zest, and ¼ teaspoon of the salt. Add the shrimp, tossing to coat well.

3. In a large nonstick skillet, heat the oil until hot but not smoking over medium heat. Add the carrot, bell pepper, and squash and cook, stirring, until the vegetables are crisp-tender, about 3 minutes. Add the shrimp and broccoli and cook, stirring, until the shrimp is almost opaque throughout, about 3 minutes.

4. Add the clam juice, lemon juice, and the remaining ½ teaspoon salt and bring to a boil. Stir in the cornstarch mixture and cook, stirring, until slightly thickened, about 1 minute. Toss with the pasta, divide among 4 plates, and serve.

Helpful hint: Remember that angel hair, the finest of all pasta strands, cooks very quickly: Depending on the brand, the pasta may be done in as little as 2 minutes.

FAT: 6G/16%
CALORIES: 342
SATURATED FAT: 0.9G
CARBOHYDRATE: 45G
PROTEIN: 28G
CHOLESTEROL: 140MG
SODIUM: 706MG

SESAME-LEMON SHRIMP STIR-FRY

SERVES: 4
WORKING TIME: 35 MINUTES
TOTAL TIME: 35 MINUTES PLUS MARINATING TIME

3 tablespoons reduced-sodium soy sauce

3 tablespoons fresh lemon juice

1 teaspoon dark Oriental sesame oil

1 teaspoon cornstarch

1 teaspoon sugar

1 pound medium shrimp, shelled and deveined

1 tablespoon vegetable oil

4 scallions, cut into 1-inch lengths

2 cloves garlic, finely chopped

1 tablespoon chopped fresh ginger

½ pound green beans, cut on the diagonal into 1-inch lengths

½ pound mushrooms, quartered

¼ teaspoon salt

½ cup canned sliced water chestnuts

¾ teaspoon grated lemon zest

1. In a medium bowl, combine the soy sauce, lemon juice, sesame oil, cornstarch, and sugar. Add the shrimp, tossing to coat well. Cover and refrigerate for at least 30 minutes or for up to 2 hours.

2. In a large nonstick skillet, heat the vegetable oil until hot but not smoking over medium heat. Add the scallions, garlic, and ginger and stir-fry until softened, about 1 minute. Add the green beans, mushrooms, and salt and stir-fry until the green beans are crisp-tender, about 4 minutes.

3. Reserving the marinade, add the shrimp to the pan along with the water chestnuts and lemon zest and stir-fry until the shrimp are almost opaque, about 4 minutes. Add the marinade and cook, stirring, until the shrimp are opaque throughout and the sauce is slightly thickened, about 1 minute.

Helpful hint: Don't marinate the shrimp for more than two hours in the hope that it will intensify the flavor. The acid in the lemon juice will turn the shrimp mushy if it soaks in it too long.

FAT: 6G/27%
CALORIES: 204
SATURATED FAT: 0.9G
CARBOHYDRATE: 16G
PROTEIN: 22G
CHOLESTEROL: 140MG
SODIUM: 732MG

Chinese methods of cooking shrimp range from the simple to the highly complex. Somewhere in between are tempting stir-fries like this one: The shrimp are marinated in a tangy sauce, then stir-fried with gentle spices and crunchy green beans and water chestnuts. Accompany the dish with rice, or break with tradition and serve a sliced baguette or breadsticks.

INDIAN-STYLE SAUTÉED COD STEAKS

SERVES: 4
WORKING TIME: 20 MINUTES
TOTAL TIME: 30 MINUTES

We tend to think of curry powder as the quintessential Indian seasoning, but in fact there is actually a myriad of styles and variations of Indian spice mixtures—some are hot, others mild— each suited to different foods. Here, a mildly hot mixture of paprika, ginger, cumin, and cayenne pepper is rubbed onto the cod steaks and then is used to season the tangy yogurt sauce.

2 teaspoons paprika

1¼ teaspoons ground cumin

½ teaspoon ground ginger

¼ teaspoon cayenne pepper

1 cup plain nonfat yogurt

1 cup small cherry tomatoes, halved

½ cup frozen baby peas, thawed

3 scallions, thinly sliced

1 tablespoon fresh lemon juice

½ teaspoon salt

4 cod steaks (about 6 ounces each), any visible bones removed

2 tablespoons flour

1 tablespoon olive oil

1. In a medium bowl, combine the paprika, cumin, ginger, and cayenne. Remove 2 teaspoons of the mixture and set aside. Add the yogurt, tomatoes, peas, scallions, lemon juice, and salt to the spice mixture in the bowl. Stir to combine.

2. Rub the reserved spice mixture onto both sides of the cod steaks. Place the flour on a sheet of waxed paper. Dredge the cod in the flour, shaking off the excess. In a large nonstick skillet, heat the oil until hot but not smoking over medium heat. Add the cod and cook until lightly browned and just opaque, about 4 minutes per side. Place on 4 plates, spoon the yogurt sauce over, and serve.

Helpful hint: Haddock or pollock steaks can be substituted for cod; these fish may be slightly softer than cod, so be extra careful when turning the steaks.

FAT: 5G/20%
CALORIES: 231
SATURATED FAT: 0.8G
CARBOHYDRATE: 13G
PROTEIN: 32G
CHOLESTEROL: 66MG
SODIUM: 435MG

CRAB CAKES WITH SPICY MANGO-MUSTARD SAUCE

SERVES: 4
WORKING TIME: 30 MINUTES
TOTAL TIME: 35 MINUTES

The use of mango chutney makes these crab cakes unique. Serve them with sautéed zucchini sticks—a healthy alternative to fries.

¾ pound lump crabmeat, picked over to remove any cartilage

6 tablespoons flour

¾ cup finely diced red bell pepper

¼ cup fresh lemon juice

¼ cup mango chutney

1 tablespoon plus 2 teaspoons Dijon mustard

1 teaspoon curry powder

½ teaspoon Worcestershire sauce

2 egg whites, lightly beaten

1 tablespoon olive oil

⅓ cup canned crushed pineapple

⅛ teaspoon cayenne pepper

1. In a medium bowl, combine the crabmeat, 2 tablespoons of the flour, ½ cup of the bell pepper, 1 tablespoon of the lemon juice, 1 tablespoon of the chutney, 2 teaspoons of the mustard, the curry powder, and Worcestershire sauce. Fold in the egg whites. Shape the mixture into 4 patties. Place the remaining ¼ cup flour on a sheet of waxed paper. Dredge the crab cakes in the flour, shaking off the excess.

2. In a large nonstick skillet, heat the oil until hot but not smoking over medium heat. Add the crab cakes, reduce the heat to medium-low, and cook until golden brown and cooked through, about 4 minutes per side.

3. Meanwhile, in a small bowl, combine the pineapple, cayenne, the remaining 3 tablespoons chutney, remaining 3 tablespoons lemon juice, remaining ¼ cup bell pepper, and remaining 1 tablespoon mustard. Divide the crab cakes among 4 plates. Top with the mango-mustard sauce and serve.

Helpful hint: Lump crabmeat consists of large, meaty chunks of cooked meat. It is available both fresh and canned. You can use either variety for this recipe, although fresh is preferable.

FAT: 5G/18%
CALORIES: 247
SATURATED FAT: 0.7G
CARBOHYDRATE: 27G
PROTEIN: 21G
CHOLESTEROL: 85MG
SODIUM: 600MG

SHRIMP-FRIED RICE

SERVES: 4
WORKING TIME: 35 MINUTES
TOTAL TIME: 50 MINUTES

1 cup long-grain rice

½ teaspoon salt

2 egg whites

1 whole egg, lightly beaten

3 tablespoons reduced-sodium soy sauce

1 tablespoon rice vinegar

1 tablespoon vegetable oil

3 cups thinly sliced leeks, white and tender green parts only

3 ribs celery, thinly sliced on the diagonal

1 red bell pepper, cut into ¼-inch squares

2 tablespoons minced fresh ginger

2 cloves garlic, minced

½ pound medium shrimp, shelled, deveined, and halved crosswise

½ pound snow peas, halved on the diagonal

¼ cup reduced-sodium chicken broth, defatted

1. In a medium saucepan, bring 2¼ cups of water to a boil. Add the rice and ¼ teaspoon of the salt, reduce to a simmer, cover, and cook until the rice is tender, about 17 minutes.

2. In a small bowl, beat together the egg whites, whole egg, soy sauce, vinegar, and the remaining ¼ teaspoon salt. Set aside.

3. In a large nonstick skillet or wok, heat 2 teaspoons of the oil until hot but not smoking over medium-high heat. Add the leeks, celery, bell pepper, ginger, and garlic and stir-fry until the vegetables are crisp-tender, 3 to 4 minutes. With a slotted spoon, transfer the vegetables to a plate. Add the remaining 1 teaspoon oil to the skillet. Add the shrimp and snow peas and stir-fry until the shrimp are just beginning to turn pink, 2 to 3 minutes.

4. Stir the egg mixture into the skillet and cook, stirring, until the egg mixture is set, about 1 minute. Return the vegetables to the skillet along with the cooked rice and the broth. Cook, stirring, until the ingredients are well combined and the shrimp are opaque throughout, about 1 minute. Divide among 4 bowls and serve.

Helpful hint: Thinly sliced scallions (both the white and green parts) can be substituted for the leeks.

FAT: 6G/15%
CALORIES: 370
SATURATED FAT: 1.1G
CARBOHYDRATE: 58G
PROTEIN: 20G
CHOLESTEROL: 124MG
SODIUM: 923MG

We've cut the fat from traditional fried rice here by omitting two egg yolks and using just 1 tablespoon of oil.

THAI-STYLE SALMON

SERVES: 4
WORKING TIME: 25 MINUTES
TOTAL TIME: 30 MINUTES

1 cup jasmine or long-grain rice

½ teaspoon salt

4 salmon steaks (about 5 ounces each), any visible bones removed

1 tablespoon fresh lime juice

2 tablespoons flour

1 tablespoon olive oil

1 red bell pepper, cut into julienne strips

1 green bell pepper, cut into julienne strips

1 small red onion, halved and thinly sliced

1 tablespoon finely chopped fresh ginger

1 cup bottled clam juice, or reduced-sodium chicken broth, defatted

3 tablespoons chili sauce

½ teaspoon grated lime zest

⅛ teaspoon red pepper flakes

⅓ cup chopped fresh basil

¼ cup chopped fresh mint

1. In a medium saucepan, bring 2¼ cups of water to a boil. Add the rice and ¼ teaspoon of the salt, reduce to a simmer, cover, and cook until the rice is tender, about 17 minutes.

2. Meanwhile, sprinkle the salmon on both sides with the lime juice. Place the flour on a sheet of waxed paper. Dredge the salmon in the flour, shaking off the excess. In a large nonstick skillet, heat the oil until hot but not smoking over medium heat. Add the salmon and cook until lightly crisped and just opaque, about 3 minutes per side. With a slotted spoon or spatula, transfer the salmon to a plate and cover loosely with foil to keep warm.

3. Add the bell peppers, onion, and ginger to the pan and cook, stirring, until the bell peppers are crisp-tender, about 3 minutes. Stir in the clam juice, chili sauce, lime zest, red pepper flakes, and the remaining ¼ teaspoon salt. Bring to a boil and cook until slightly thickened, about 3 minutes. Stir in the basil and mint. Divide the rice among 4 plates. Serve the salmon alongside, topped with the sauce.

Helpful hint: If you can't find jasmine rice (now grown in the United States as well as Thailand), look for Texmati, a reasonably priced Texas-grown rice similar to basmati.

FAT: 12G/25%
CALORIES: 433
SATURATED FAT: 1.8G
CARBOHYDRATE: 50G
PROTEIN: 30G
CHOLESTEROL: 69MG
SODIUM: 635MG

148

Salmon is often treated gently—poached and served with a creamy sauce. The Thai way with fish is bolder, using tart flavors like citrus juice and zest, hot chilies, and aromatic herbs. Here, the salmon is topped with peppers and onion cooked with ginger, lime, and chili sauce. Jasmine rice, a fragrant Thai variety, tastes much like Indian basmati rice but costs less.

SCALLOPS WITH ASIAN VEGETABLES AND NOODLES

SERVES: 4
WORKING TIME: 30 MINUTES
TOTAL TIME: 30 MINUTES

While it may look complicated, this Asian-inspired pasta-and-seafood dish is a snap to prepare: You can make the marinade and begin stir-frying while the pasta is cooking. The finished dish is filled with subtle variations of taste and texture— the smoky bacon sets off the sweet scallops, while the tender linguine is a foil for the crisp vegetables.

8 ounces linguine

½ cup reduced-sodium chicken broth, defatted

3 tablespoons reduced-sodium soy sauce

3 tablespoons dry sherry

1½ teaspoons cornstarch

1 teaspoon dark Oriental sesame oil

½ teaspoon ground ginger

1 pound bay scallops or quartered sea scallops

1 tablespoon vegetable oil

3 tablespoons slivered Canadian bacon (1 ounce)

¼ teaspoon red pepper flakes

1 red bell pepper, slivered

6 ounces snow peas, strings removed

1½ cups bean sprouts

1. In a large pot of boiling water, cook the linguine until just tender. Drain well.

2. Meanwhile, in a small bowl, combine the broth, soy sauce, sherry, cornstarch, sesame oil, and ginger. Add the scallops, tossing to coat.

3. In a large nonstick skillet or wok, heat the vegetable oil until hot but not smoking over medium heat. Add the Canadian bacon and red pepper flakes and stir-fry until the bacon is lightly crisped, about 2 minutes. Add the bell pepper and stir-fry until crisp-tender, about 3 minutes.

4. Reserving the marinade, add the scallops to the pan along with the linguine, snow peas, and bean sprouts and cook, stirring, until the scallops are cooked through and the linguine is piping hot, about 4 minutes. Stir the marinade to recombine, pour into the skillet and cook, stirring, until slightly thickened, about 1 minute.

Helpful hint: There's quite a variety of sprouts on the market these days, from threadlike radish and alfalfa sprouts to the familiar thick, crunchy bean sprouts. Use a mixture, if you like.

FAT: 7G/15%
CALORIES: 425
SATURATED FAT: 1G
CARBOHYDRATE: 55G
PROTEIN: 31G
CHOLESTEROL: 41MG
SODIUM: 823MG

SCALLOPS WITH ORANGE SAUCE

SERVES: 4
WORKING TIME: 30 MINUTES
TOTAL TIME: 30 MINUTES

While scallops may seem like something of a luxury, they justify their cost by their convenience (there's nothing to shuck, clean, or fillet) and, of course, by their inimitable flavor. Here, bay scallops are dredged with flour to give them a crisp coating when stir-fried; the tarragon-scented sauce is based on orange juice and vermouth.

1 cup long-grain rice

¾ teaspoon salt

2 tablespoons flour

1 pound bay scallops or quartered sea scallops

4 teaspoons olive oil

2 red bell peppers, slivered

3 shallots, finely chopped, or ¼ cup chopped scallions

½ cup dry vermouth

½ teaspoon grated orange zest

1 cup orange juice

¾ teaspoon dried tarragon

2 teaspoons cornstarch mixed with 1 tablespoon water

¼ cup chopped fresh parsley

1. In a medium saucepan, bring 2¼ cups of water to a boil. Add the rice and ¼ teaspoon of the salt, reduce to a simmer, cover, and cook until the rice is tender, about 17 minutes.

2. In a sturdy plastic bag, combine the flour and ¼ teaspoon of the salt. Add the scallops to the bag, shaking to coat with the flour mixture. In a large nonstick skillet or wok, heat the oil until hot but not smoking over medium heat. Add the scallops and stir-fry until not quite opaque in the center, about 1 minute. With a slotted spoon, transfer the scallops to a plate.

3. Add the bell peppers and shallots to the skillet and stir-fry until softened, about 3 minutes. Add the vermouth, increase the heat to high, and cook, stirring, until reduced by half, about 1 minute. Add the orange zest, orange juice, tarragon, and the remaining ¼ teaspoon salt and bring to a boil. Add the cornstarch mixture and cook, stirring, until slightly thickened, about 1 minute. Reduce the heat to low, return the scallops to the pan, and cook just until the scallops are opaque throughout, about 1 minute. Divide the rice among 4 plates. Spoon the scallop mixture over, sprinkle with the parsley, and serve.

Helpful hint: Vermouth is a fortified wine made aromatic by infusion with herbs, spices, barks, and flowers. You can substitute dry white wine, if you like.

FAT: 6G/13%
CALORIES: 411
SATURATED FAT: 0.8G
CARBOHYDRATE: 56G
PROTEIN: 24G
CHOLESTEROL: 38MG
SODIUM: 604MG

GLOSSARY

Asparagus—A delicate stalk vegetable that appears in late spring. Select firm, straight, medium-thick spears that have tightly closed buds at the tips and moist, green bases. Since asparagus is grown in sandy soil, it should be rinsed well, especially the tips. Snap off the tough bottoms from the stems and, if necessary, peel the lower part of the stalks with a vegetable peeler. If refrigerating asparagus for a day or two, stand the stalks in a container with about ½ inch of cool water, and cover the tips with a plastic bag.

Basil—A highly fragrant herb with a flavor somewhere between licorice and cloves. Like many fresh herbs, basil will retain more of its taste if added at the end of cooking; dried basil is quite flavorful and can stand up to longer cooking. Store fresh basil by placing the stems in a container of water and covering the leaves loosely with a plastic bag.

Canadian bacon—A lean smoked meat, similar to ham. This bacon is precooked, so it can be used as is. (For extra flavor, cook it in a skillet until the edges are lightly crisped.) Just a small amount adds big flavor to stir-fries and other dishes, but with much less fat than regular bacon.

Capers—The flower buds of a small bush found in Mediterranean countries. To make capers, the buds are dried and then pickled in vinegar with some salt: To reduce saltiness, rinse before using. The piquant taste of capers permeates any sauce quickly, and just a few supply a big flavor boost.

Cayenne pepper—A hot spice ground from dried red chili peppers. Add cayenne to taste when preparing Mexican, Tex-Mex, Indian, Chinese, and Caribbean dishes; start with just a small amount, as cayenne is fiery-hot.

Chili powder—A commercially prepared seasoning mixture made from ground dried chilies, oregano, cumin, coriander, salt, and dehydrated garlic, and sometimes cloves and allspice. Use in chilis, sauces, and spice rubs for a Southwestern punch. Chili powders can range in strength from mild to very hot; for proper potency, use within 6 months of purchase. Pure ground chili powder, without any added spices, is also available.

Chop—To roughly cut an ingredient into small pieces—not as uniform as dicing and not as fine as mincing. The flavor of the ingredient will permeate the dish, and a hint of texture will remain. To chop, anchor the back of the knife-tip (a chef's knife is best) with your hand, and quickly lift and lower the handle, slowly moving the blade across the food.

Cilantro/Coriander—A lacy-leaved green herb (called by both names). The plant's seeds are dried and used as a spice (known as coriander). The fresh herb, much used in Mexican and Asian cooking, looks like pale flat-leaf parsley and is strongly aromatic. Store fresh cilantro by placing the stems in a container of water and covering the leaves loosely with a plastic bag. Coriander seeds are important in Mexican and Indian cuisines; sold whole or ground, they have a somewhat citrusy flavor that complements both sweet and savory dishes.

Cornstarch—A fine flour made from the germ of the corn. Cornstarch, like flour, is used as a fat-free sauce thickener; cornstarch-thickened sauces are lighter, glossier, and more translucent than those made with flour. To prevent lumps, combine the cornstarch with a cold liquid before adding it to

a hot sauce; bring it gently to a boil and don't stir too vigorously, or the sauce may thin.

Cumin—A pungent, peppery-tasting spice essential to many Middle Eastern, Asian, Mexican, and Mediterranean dishes. Available ground or as whole seeds; the spice can be toasted in a dry skillet to bring out its flavor.

Curry powder—Not one spice but a mix of spices, commonly used in Indian cooking to flavor a dish with sweet heat and add a characteristic yellow-orange color. While curry blends vary (consisting of as many as 20 herbs and spices) they typically include turmeric (for its vivid yellow color), fenugreek, ginger, cardamom, cloves, cumin, coriander, and cayenne pepper. Commercially available Madras curry is hotter than other store-bought types.

Dice—To cut food into small, uniform squares of ⅛ to ¼ inch, adding visual interest and texture to a dish. To dice, cut the ingredient into uniform strips, depending on how small or large you want the dice. Then cut the strips crosswise.

Dill—A name given to both the fresh herb and the small, hard seeds that are used as a spice. Add the light, lemony, fresh dill leaves (also called dillweed) toward the end of cooking. Dill seeds provide a pleasantly distinctive bitter taste and marry beautifully with sour cream- or yogurt-based sauces.

Evaporated milk, skimmed and low-fat—Canned, unsweetened, homogenized milk that has had most of its fat removed: In the skimmed version, 100 percent of the fat has been removed; the low-fat version contains 1 percent fat. Used in sauces, these products add a creamy richness with almost no fat. Store at room temperature for up to 6 months until opened, then refrigerate for up to 1 week.

Flour, all-purpose—A refined wheat flour, made from a blend of hard and soft wheats, that is suitable for most cooking purposes. Also called plain flour, all-purpose flour comes bleached or unbleached; use whichever you prefer (the bleaching has no effect on the finished product).

Garlic—The edible bulb of a plant closely related to onions, leeks, and chives. Garlic can be pungently assertive or sweetly mild, depending on how it is prepared: Minced or crushed garlic yields a more powerful flavor than whole or halved cloves. Whereas sautéing or stir-frying turns garlic rich and savory, slow simmering or roasting produces a mild, mellow flavor. Select firm, plump bulbs with dry skins; avoid bulbs that have begun to sprout. Store garlic in an open or loosely covered container in a cool, dark place for up to 2 months.

Ginger, fresh—A thin-skinned root used as a seasoning. Fresh ginger adds sweet pungency to Asian and Indian dishes. Tightly wrapped, unpeeled fresh ginger can be refrigerated for 1 week or frozen for up to 6 months.

Honey—A liquid sweetener made by honeybees from flower nectar. It ranges in flavor from mild (orange blossom) to very strong (buckwheat). Deliciously versatile, honey adds mellow sweetness to savory dishes. Store honey at room temperature. If it crystallizes, place the open jar in a pan of warm water for a few minutes; or microwave it for 10 to 15 seconds, or until the honey liquefies.

Hot pepper sauce—A highly incendiary sauce made from a variety of hot peppers flavored with vinegar and salt. This sauce comes into play in Caribbean dishes as well as in Creole, Cajun, and other southern cuisines. Use sparingly, drop by drop, to introduce a hot edge to any dish.

Juice, citrus—The flavorful liquid component of oranges, lemon, limes, tangerines, and the like. Freshly squeezed citrus juice has an inimitable freshness that livens up low-fat foods; Chinese and Thai stir-fries often feature citrus-based sauces. Frozen juice concentrates make a tangy base for sweet or savory sauces. An inexpensive hand reamer makes quick work of juicing citrus fruits.

Julienne—Thin, uniform, matchstick-size pieces of an ingredient, usually a vegetable, typically 2 inches long. To form julienne, cut the food into long, thin slices; stack the slices and cut them lengthwise into sticks, then trim them crosswise into the desired length.

Leek—A mild-flavored member of the onion family that resembles a giant scallion. Buy leeks with firm bottoms and fresh-looking tops; store them, loosely wrapped in plastic, in the refrigerator. To prepare, trim the root end and any blemished dark green ends. Split the leek lengthwise, then rinse thoroughly to remove any dirt trapped between the leaves.

Mince—To cut an ingredient into very small pieces (finer than chopping), so its flavor infuses the dish and the pieces themselves practically disappear when cooked. Mincing is usually used with foods that provide background flavor, such as scallions, garlic, ginger, and onions. The technique of rocking the knife handle while stabilizing the blade-tip on the work surface is the same as for chopping.

Mint—A large family of herbs used to impart a refreshingly heady fragrance and cool aftertaste to foods; the most common types are spearmint and peppermint. As with other fresh herbs, mint is best added toward the end of the cooking time. Store fresh mint the same way as fresh cilantro.

Olive oil—A fragrant oil pressed from olives. This oil is rich in monounsaturated fats, which make it more healthful than butter and other solid shortenings. Olive oil comes in different grades, reflecting the method used to refine the oil and the resulting level of acidity. The finest, most expensive oil is cold-pressed extra-virgin, which should be reserved for flavoring salad dressings and other uncooked or lightly cooked foods. "Virgin" and "pure" olive oils are slightly more acidic with less olive flavor, and are fine for most types of cooking.

Paprika—A spice ground from a variety of red peppers and used in many traditional Hungarian and Spanish dishes and is used in other cuisines as well. Paprika colors foods a characteristic brick-red and flavors dishes from sweet to spicy-hot, depending on the pepper potency. Like all pepper-based spices, paprika loses its color and flavor with time; check your supply and replace it if necessary.

Parsley—A popular herb available in two varieties. Curly parsley, with lacy, frilly leaves, is quite mild and is preferred for garnishing, while flat-leaf Italian parsley has a stronger flavor and is better for cooking. Store parsley as you would basil. Since fresh parsley is so widely available, there is really no reason to use dried, which has very little flavor.

Parsnip—A beige-colored winter root vegetable that becomes nutty and almost sweet when cooked. To prepare for cooking, simply peel and cut into slices or julienne strips for adding to stir-fries and sautés. Refrigerate parsnips, unwashed, in a perforated plastic bag for up to 1 week, or longer if they remain firm.

Pine nuts—The seeds of certain pine trees that grow in several parts of the world, including Italy and Mexico. Called pignoli or pinoli in Italian, they are best known for their role in pesto, the classic basil sauce for pasta; they're also used in Chinese dishes. Use pine nuts sparingly, since they are high in fat. Look for them in the Italian foods or nuts section of your market. Store the nuts in a tightly closed jar in the freezer for up to 6 months. Toast pine nuts briefly before using to bring out their full flavor.

Rice, long-grain—A type of rice with grains much longer than they are wide. Long-grain rice remains fluffy and separate when cooked. Converted rice, which has been specially processed to preserve nutrients, takes slightly longer to cook than regular white rice. Rice is ideal for low-fat cooking since it absorbs other flavors and is quite filling, yet it contributes almost no fat; it's the perfect companion for Asian-style stir-fries.

Sherry—A fortified wine, originally made in Spain but now produced elsewhere as well. Sherries range in sweetness from quite dry (labeled *fino, manzanillo,* or simply "dry") to medium-dry (labeled *amontillado* or "milk sherry") to sweet (*oloroso,* also called "cream" or "golden"). Use a dry sherry to add a fragrant bouquet to savory sauces.

Sour cream—A soured dairy product, resulting from treating sweet cream with a lactic acid culture. In savory sautés, sour cream adds tangy flavor and creamy richness to the sauce. Regular sour cream contains at least 18 percent milk fat by volume; reduced-fat sour cream contains 4 percent fat; nonfat sour cream is, of course, fat-free. In cooking, the reduced-fat version can be substituted for regular sour cream; use the nonfat cautiously since it behaves differently. To avoid curdling, do not subject sour cream to high heat.

Soy sauce, reduced-sodium—A condiment made from fermented soybeans, wheat, and salt used to add a salty, slightly sweet flavor to food. Soy sauce is especially at home in stir-fries and other Asian-style preparations. Keep in mind that reduced-sodium sauces add the same flavor but much less sodium.

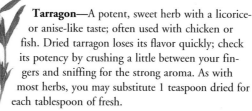

Tarragon—A potent, sweet herb with a licorice- or anise-like taste; often used with chicken or fish. Dried tarragon loses its flavor quickly; check its potency by crushing a little between your fingers and sniffing for the strong aroma. As with most herbs, you may substitute 1 teaspoon dried for each tablespoon of fresh.

Tomatoes, cherry—Round tomatoes roughly the size of ping-pong balls; may be red or yellow. Cherry tomatoes are just the right size for kebabs and can also be sautéed, whole or halved, and, of course, used in salads. Cherry tomatoes are usually sold in baskets. Choose the reddest ones you can find and store them at room temperature to preserve their flavor.

Turnip—A winter root vegetable used in sautés and stir-fries for its bittersweet flavor and slight crunch. Available all year round, turnips have a peak season from October to February. Buy small turnips, with unblemished skins, as they will have the mildest flavor.

Vinegar, balsamic—A dark red vinegar made from the unfermented juice of pressed grapes, most commonly the white Trebbiano, and aged in wooden casks. The authentic version is produced in a small region in Northern Italy, around Modena, and tastes richly sweet with a slight sour edge. Balsamic vinegar is mild and mellow, and makes a wonderful flavoring for sauces.

Vinegar, rice—A pale vinegar made from fermented rice, it is milder than most other types of vinegar. Its light, clean flavor is much favored in Asian cooking. Japanese rice vinegar is widely available; be sure to buy the unseasoned type.

Yogurt, nonfat and low-fat—Delicately tart cultured milk products made from low-fat or skim milk. Plain yogurt makes a healthful base for sauté sauces, replacing higher-fat dairy products such as sour cream or heavy cream.

Zest, citrus—The thin, outermost colored part of the rind of citrus fruits that contains strongly flavored oils. Zest imparts an intense flavor that makes a refreshing contrast to the richness of meat, poultry, or fish. Remove the zest with a

grater, citrus zester, or vegetable peeler; be careful to remove only the colored layer, not the bitter white pith beneath it.

INDEX

TIME
LIFE
BOOKS

Time-Life Books is a division of Time Life Inc.

TIME LIFE INC.
PRESIDENT and CEO: George Artandi

TIME-LIFE BOOKS
PRESIDENT: John D. Hall
PUBLISHER/MANAGING EDITOR: Neil Kagan

GREAT TASTE~LOW FAT
Stir-Fries & Sautés

DEPUTY EDITOR: Marion Ferguson Briggs
MARKETING DIRECTOR: Robin B. Shuster

Consulting Editor: Catherine Boland Hackett

Vice President, Director of Finance: Christopher Hearing
Vice President, Book Production: Marjann Caldwell
Director of Operations: Eileen Bradley
Director of Photography and Research: John Conrad Weiser
Director of Editorial Administration: Judith W. Shanks
Production Manager: Marlene Zack
Quality Assurance Manager: James King
Library: Louise D. Forstall

Design for Great Taste~Low Fat by David Fridberg of
Miles Fridberg Molinaroli, Inc.

 REBUS, INC.
PUBLISHER: Rodney M. Friedman
EDITORIAL DIRECTOR: Charles L. Mee

Editorial Staff for *Stir-Fries & Sautés*
Director, Recipe Development and Photography: Grace Young
Editorial Director: Kate Slate
Senior Recipe Developer: Sandra Rose Gluck
Recipe Developers: Helen Jones, Paul Piccuito
Writer: Bonnie J. Slotnick
Managing Editor: Julee Binder Shapiro
Editorial Assistant: James W. Brown, Jr.
Nutritionists: Hill Nutrition Associates

Art Director: Timothy Jeffs
Photographers: Corinne Colen, Edmund Goldspink, Lisa Koenig
Photographers' Assistants: Alix Berenberg, Bill Bies, Bain Coffman,
    Katie Bleacher Everard, Rainer Fehringer, Petra Liebetanz
Food Stylists: Karen Pickus, Karen Tack
Assistant Food Stylists: Charles Davis, Ellie Ritt
Prop Stylist: Debrah Donahue
Prop Coordinator: Karin Martin

Special thanks to Chantal Cookware Corporation

Library of Congress Cataloging-in-Publication Data

Stir-fries & sautés.
    p.   cm. -- (Great taste, low fat)
Includes index.
ISBN 0-7835-4561-4
1. Stir frying. 2. Low-fat diet--Recipes. 3. Quick and easy cookery.
I. Time-Life Books. II. Series.
TX689.5.S733   1996
641.7'7--dc20
                                                    96-17872
                                                        CIP

OTHER PUBLICATIONS

COOKING
WEIGHT WATCHERS® SMART CHOICE RECIPE COLLECTION
WILLIAMS-SONOMA KITCHEN LIBRARY

DO IT YOURSELF
THE TIME-LIFE COMPLETE GARDENER
HOME REPAIR AND IMPROVEMENT
THE ART OF WOODWORKING
FIX IT YOURSELF

TIME-LIFE KIDS
FAMILY TIME BIBLE STORIES
LIBRARY OF FIRST QUESTIONS AND ANSWERS
A CHILD'S FIRST LIBRARY OF LEARNING
I LOVE MATH
NATURE COMPANY DISCOVERIES
UNDERSTANDING SCIENCE & NATURE

HISTORY
THE AMERICAN STORY
VOICES OF THE CIVIL WAR
THE AMERICAN INDIANS
LOST CIVILIZATIONS
MYSTERIES OF THE UNKNOWN
TIME FRAME
THE CIVIL WAR
CULTURAL ATLAS

SCIENCE/NATURE
VOYAGE THROUGH THE UNIVERSE

*For information on and a full description of any of the Time-Life Books series
listed above, please call 1-800-621-7026 or write:*
Reader Information
Time-Life Customer Service
P.O. Box C-32068
Richmond, Virginia 23261-2068

METRIC CONVERSION CHARTS

VOLUME EQUIVALENTS
(fluid ounces/milliliters and liters)

US	Metric
1 tsp	5 ml
1 tbsp (½ fl oz)	15 ml
¼ cup (2 fl oz)	60 ml
⅓ cup	80 ml
½ cup (4 fl oz)	120 ml
⅔ cup	160 ml
¾ cup (6 fl oz)	180 ml
1 cup (8 fl oz)	240 ml
1 qt (32 fl oz)	950 ml
1 qt + 3 tbsps	1 L
1 gal (128 fl oz)	4 L

Conversion formula
Fluid ounces X 30 = milliliters
1000 milliliters = 1 liter

WEIGHT EQUIVALENTS
(ounces and pounds/grams and kilograms)

US	Metric
¼ oz	7 g
½ oz	15 g
¾ oz	20 g
1 oz	30 g
8 oz (½ lb)	225 g
12 oz (¾ lb)	340 g
16 oz (1 lb)	455 g
35 oz (2.2 lbs)	1 kg

Conversion formula
Ounces X 28.35 = grams
1000 grams = 1 kilogram

LINEAR EQUIVALENTS
(inches and feet/centimeters and meters)

US	Metric
¼ in	.75 cm
½ in	1.5 cm
¾ in	2 cm
1 in	2.5 cm
6 in	15 cm
12 in (1 ft)	30 cm
39 in	1 m

Conversion formula
Inches X 2.54 = centimeters
100 centimeters = 1 meter

TEMPERATURE EQUIVALENTS
(Fahrenheit/Celsius)

US	Metric
0° (freezer temperature)	-18°
32° (water freezes)	0°
98.6°	37°
180° (water simmers*)	82°
212° (water boils*)	100°
250° (low oven)	120°
350° (moderate oven)	175°
425° (hot oven)	220°
500° (very hot oven)	260°

*at sea level

Conversion formula
Degrees Fahrenheit minus
32 ÷ 1.8 = degrees Celsius